Nova Venus

by

MAHLON BLAINE

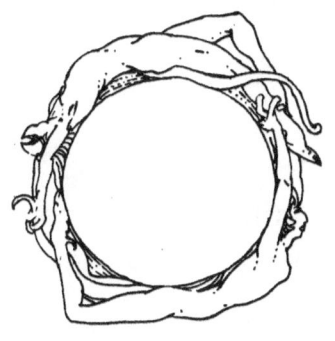

NEW YORK
1938

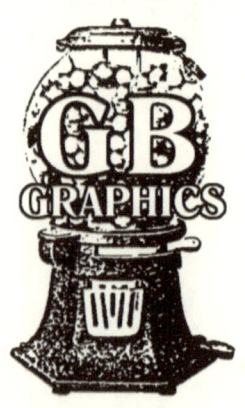

ISBN 978-1-304-60775-1

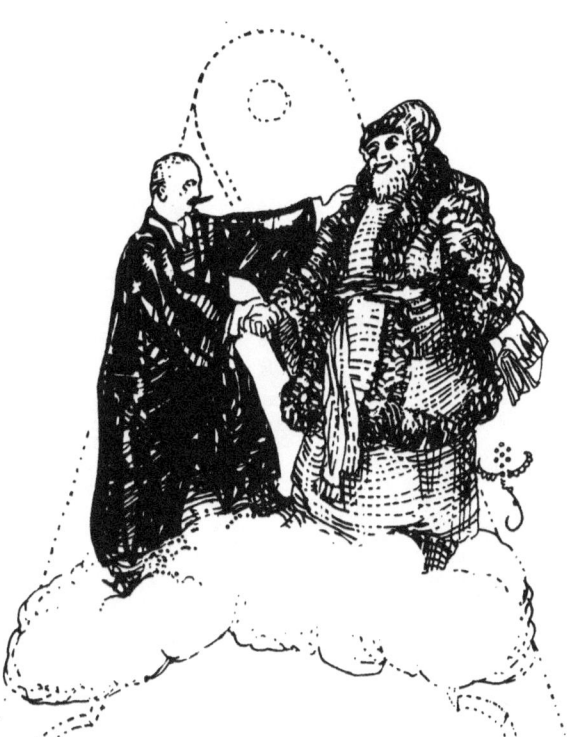

The drawings in "Nova Venus"
are dedicated to my Father-in-Law,
Fred Ezra Stivers, Esq.,
Lawyer — Judge
(who had in his inner office,
in a gold frame, a portrait of one,
François Rabelais)+

His impromptu talks on symbology, his idea
for a picture-story merging mysticism with
satire contributed more to "Nova Venus"
than is apparent. He did not live to see
these drawings published — Yet — I have a
comfortable feeling that he is looking over my
shoulder — for I seem to hear the whisper
of a learned chuckle — and — at times a
cosmic belly-laugh (which he reserved for
stories dealing with the discomforture of Hypocrites),
I feel that he walks with me — talks with me —
and what is more important — he laughs with me+

*I*NFINITELY GRACIOUS, radiantly beautiful, Aphrodite rose from the foam. All life loved and laughed, and begot new life in tender play.

"*Alma Venus genetrix!*" the poet sang.

Love became lust, laughter scorn, life a combat. Groves gave way to market places; paths worn by tranquil herds became hard-surfaced streets resounding to the clash of iron-shod hoofs and rattling chariot wheels.

"Venus of the Crossways," sighed a realist.

Love stood on the corner and simpered and bartered. In secret places merchants offered new combinations and re-combinations to tempt the cynical, cloyed with sophistication.

"Sin!" screamed the prophet. "Ye shall suffer and castigate."

The saint writhed under the lash and yearned for purity. A black cloud rose up out of hell, a tornado of maddened bodies dancing obscenely in the Witches' Sabbat to do ribald honor to the Venus of Tannhauser.

Saint and witch were methodically suppressed by a sour and sober folk. "Duty," they said, as they hanged the witch, burned the saint, and put aprons on antique statues. This last they did because they could tolerate no reminders of Eden times when life, love, laughter, and play were gentleness.

The aprons slipped. The fervor of saintliness and the fury of lust infernal had long been quenched. Now sobriety relaxed, sourness sought alkalinity.

A streamlined era (unable to impose a mechanical pattern of clarity on complex confusion), aware of all that has been, profoundly troubled by its urges yet bluffing a mastery over them, has created a deity in its own image.

She is an irreverent enchantress. An uncanny wisdom, of the world and the other worlds, lurks in her bizarrerie.

Hers is the realm where all things touch, and, touching, engender. Her magic joins neither like to like nor opposite to opposite. Under her spell the subtly inter-related incestuously inter-create the ever unexpected inevitable.

She is Nova Venus

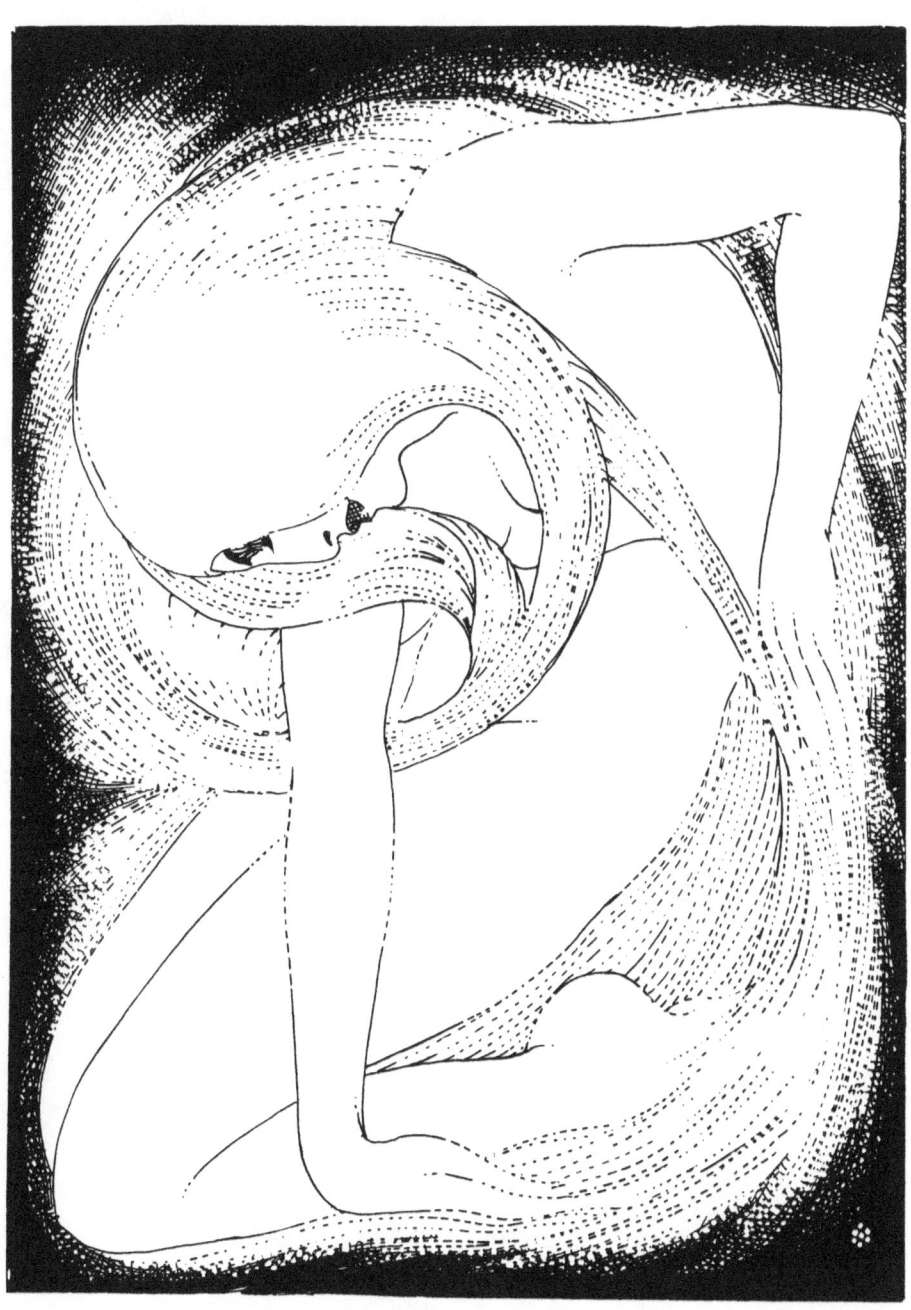

4. Infinitely gracious

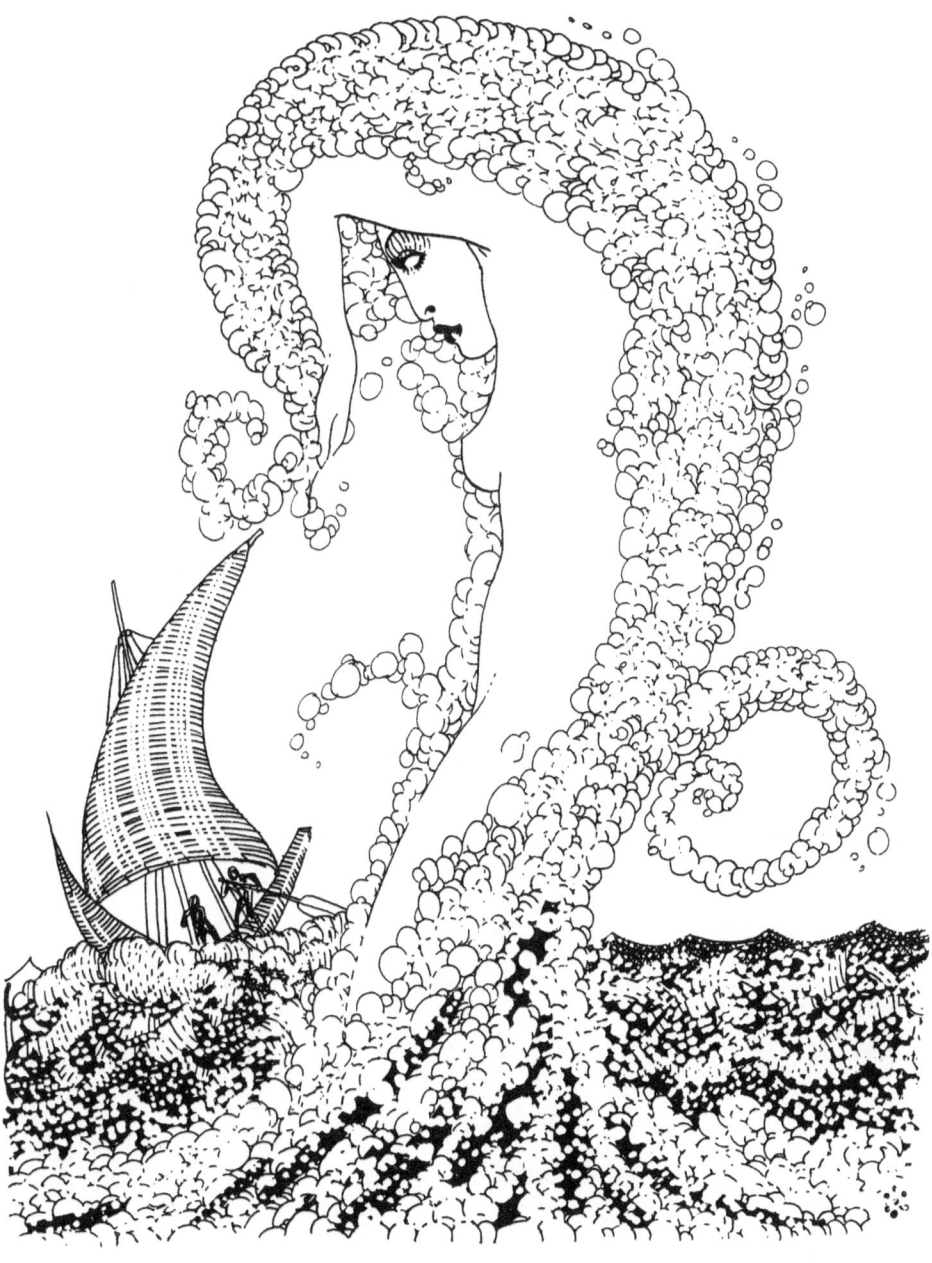

5. Radiantly beautiful, Aphrodite rose from the foam

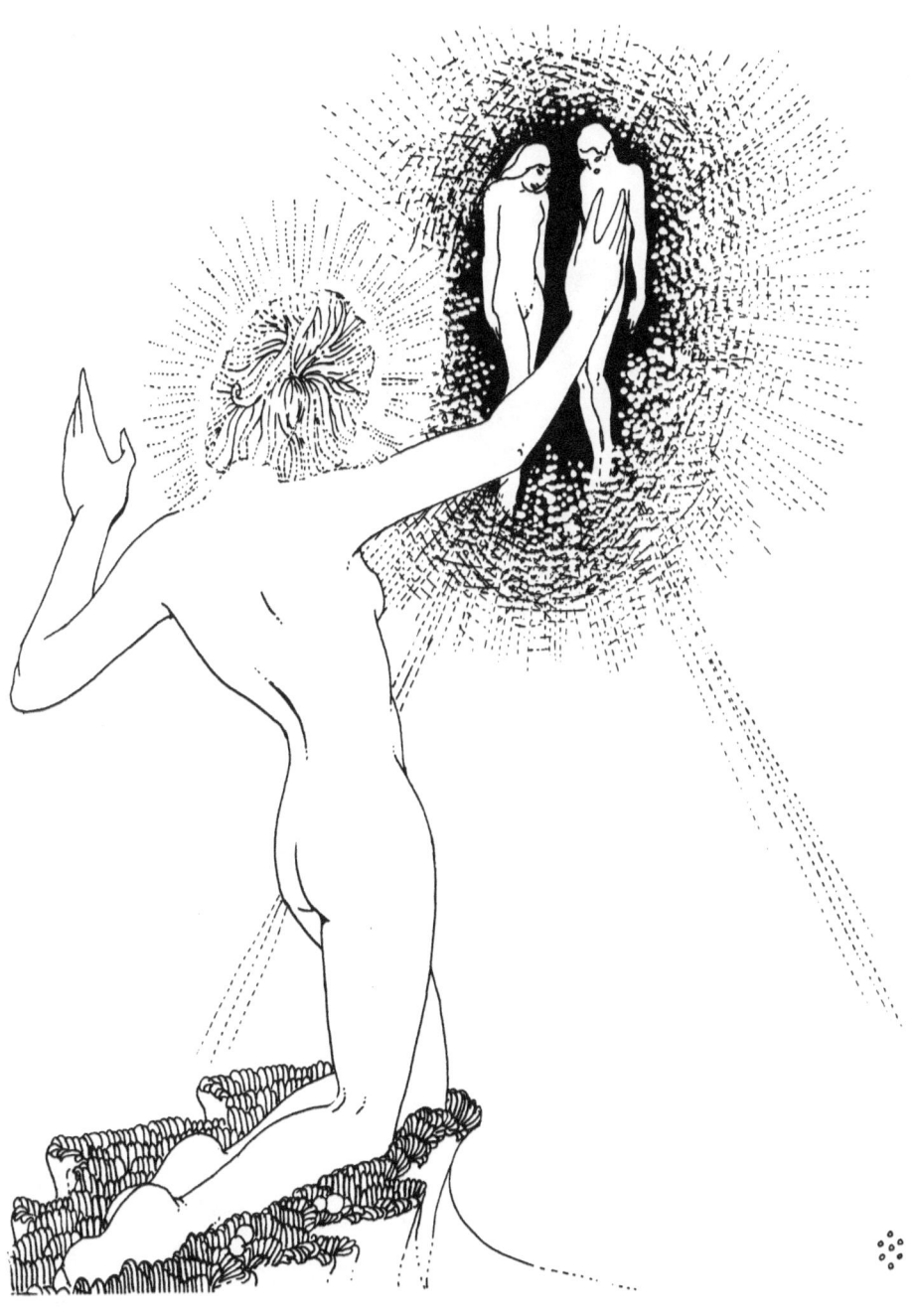

6. *And out of her bounty she created man and woman*

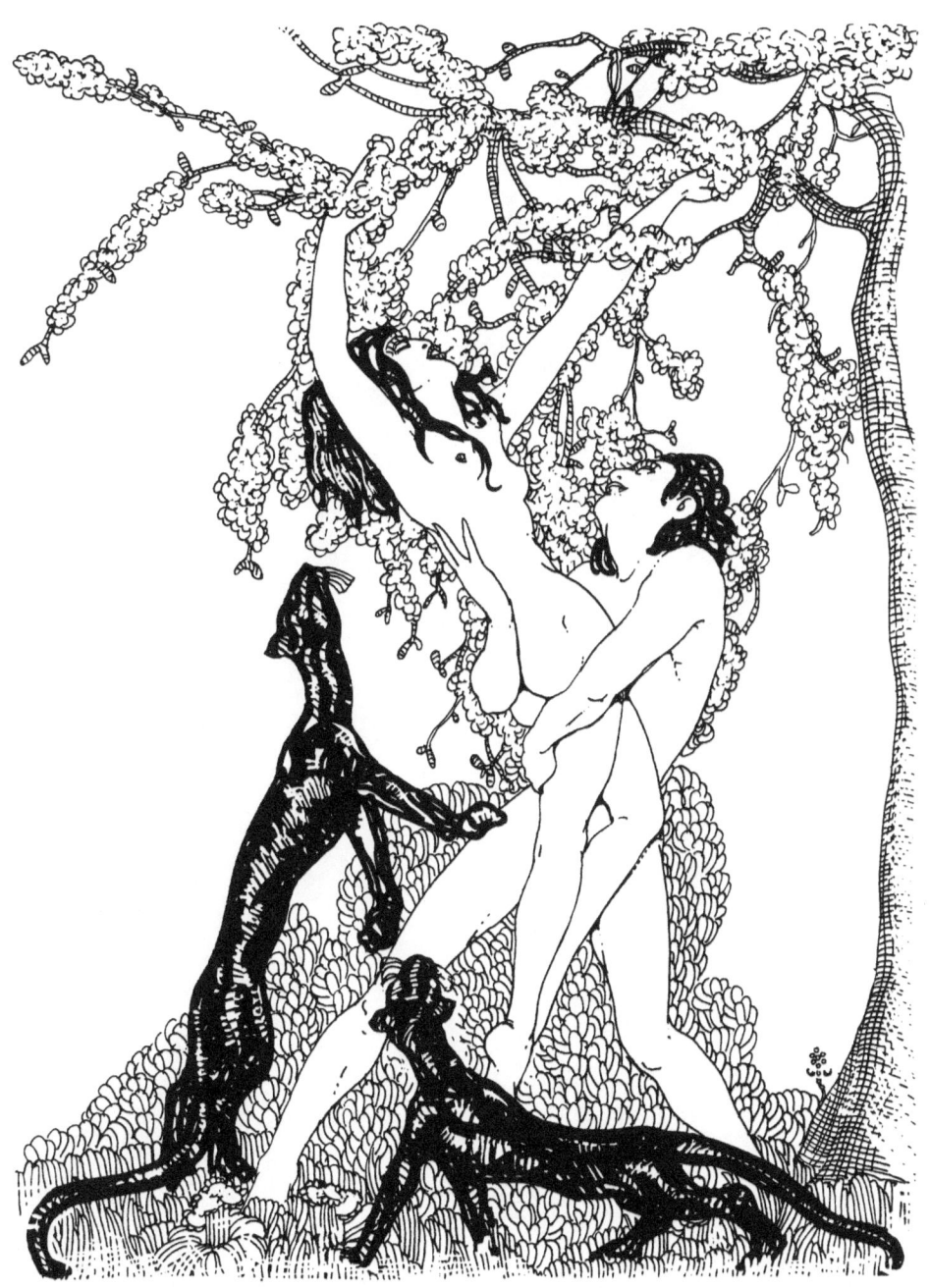

7. And all life loved and played

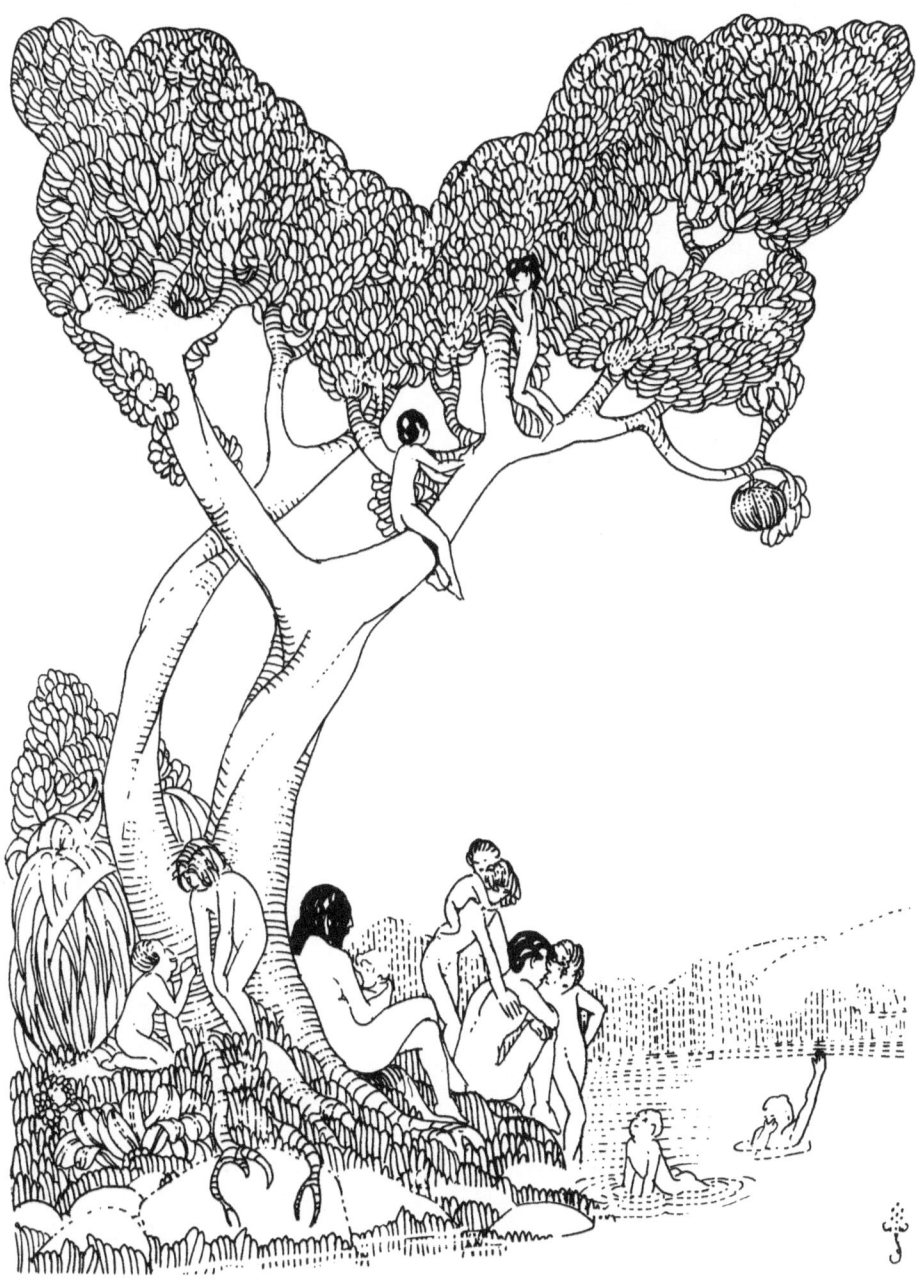

8. And begot new life in tender play

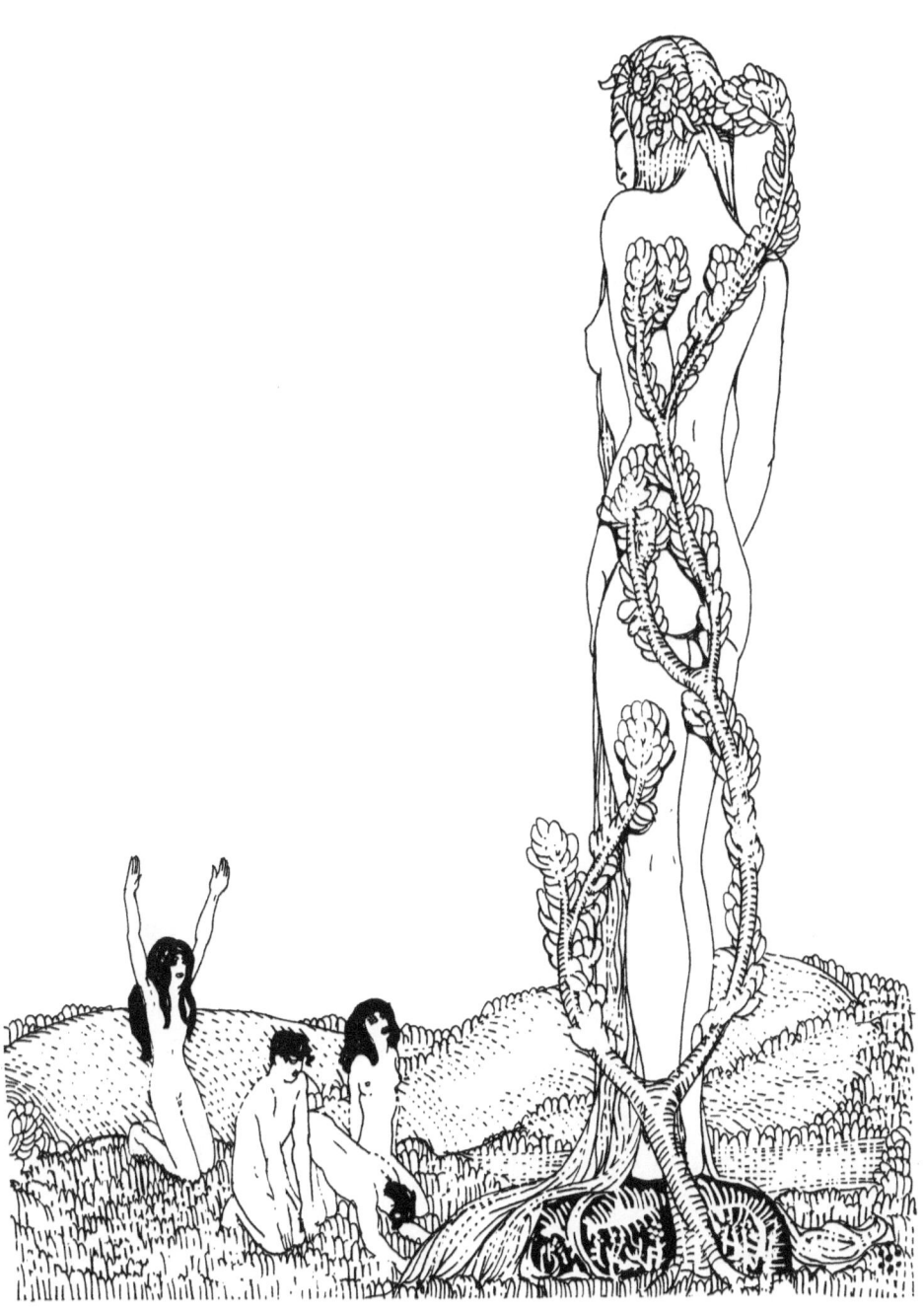

9. *And they worshipped love*

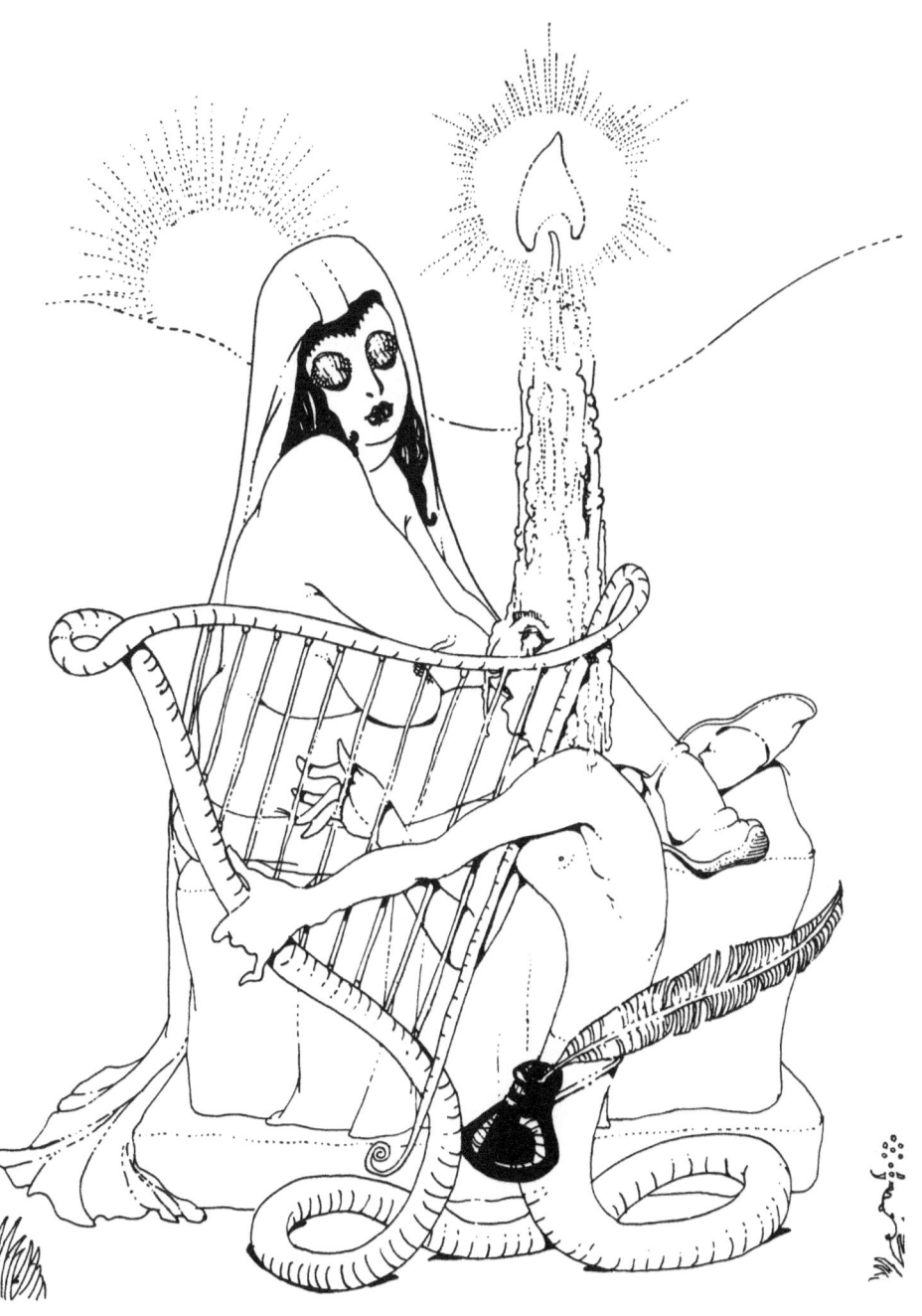

10. *"Alma Venus generix,"* the poet sang

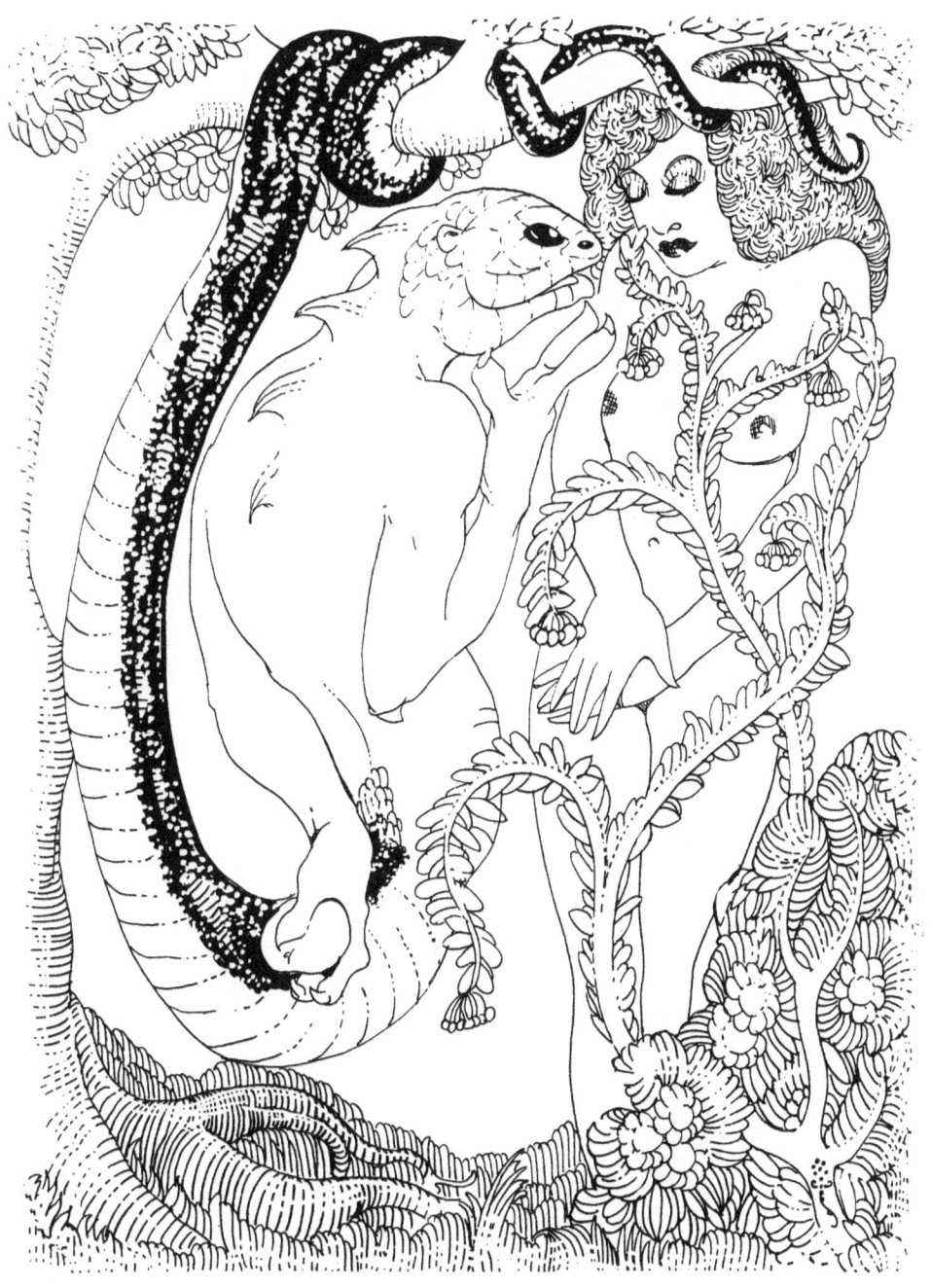

11. *But life was tempted to know*

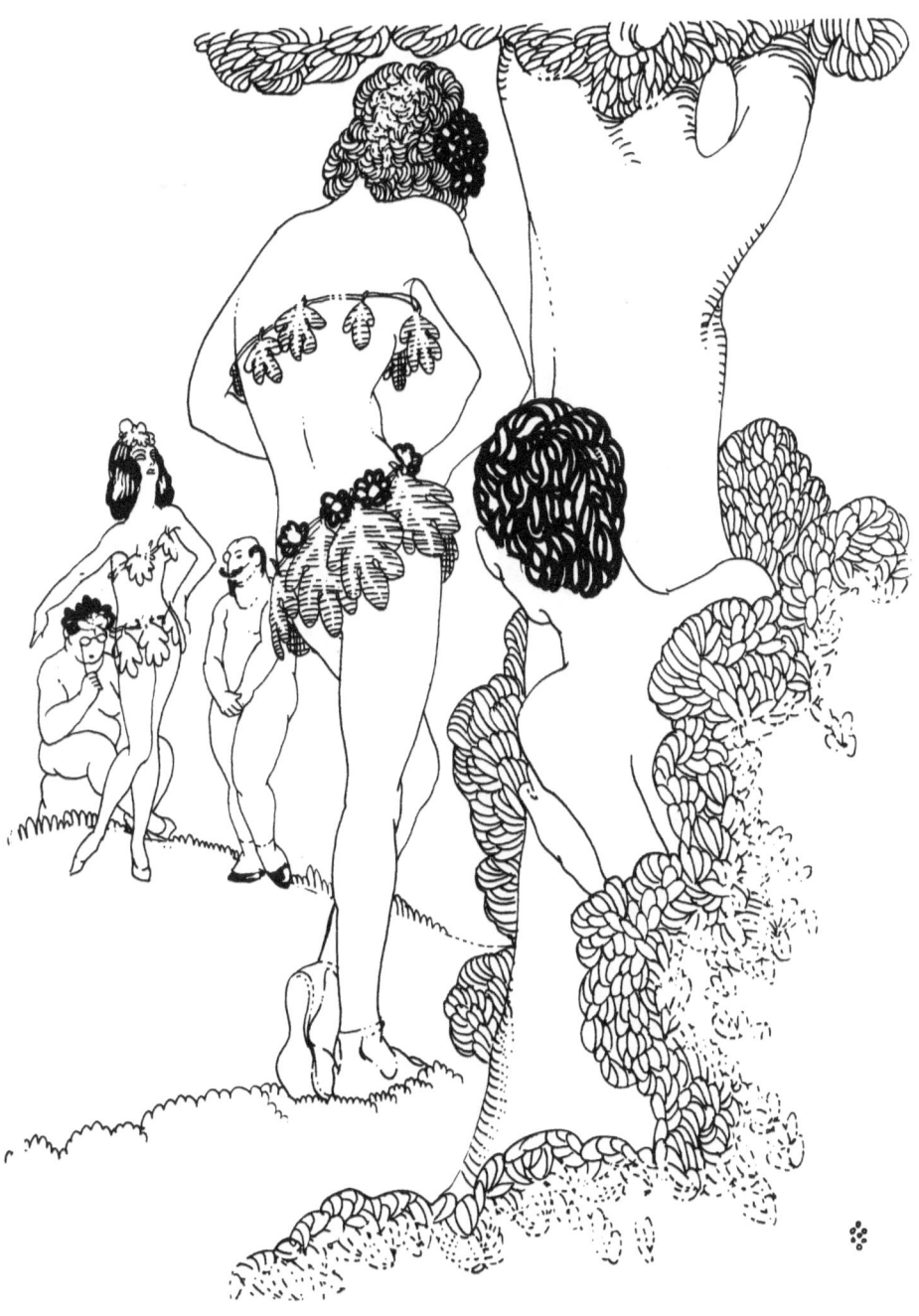

12.   *And they learnt they were naked*

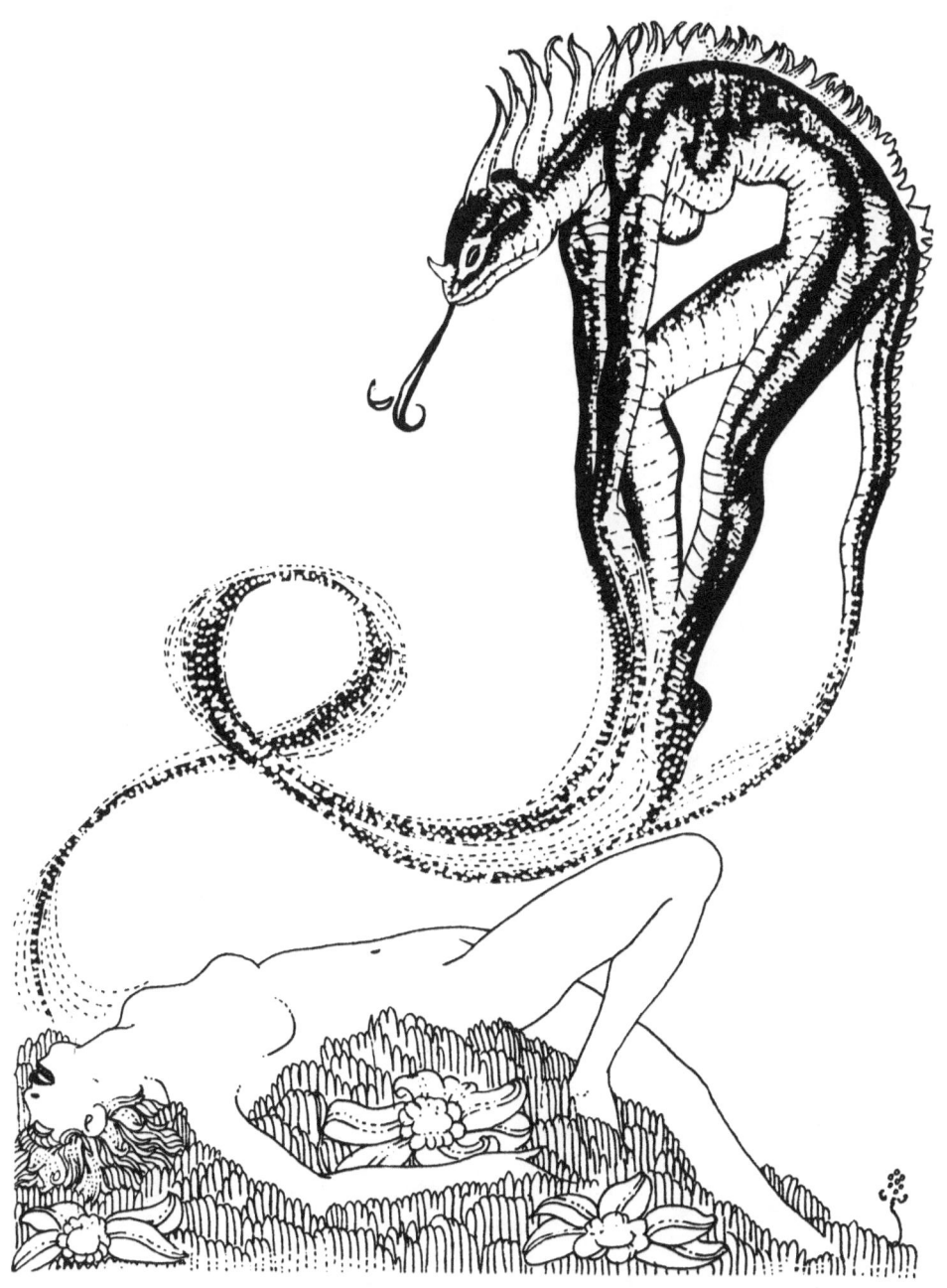

13. Love became lust

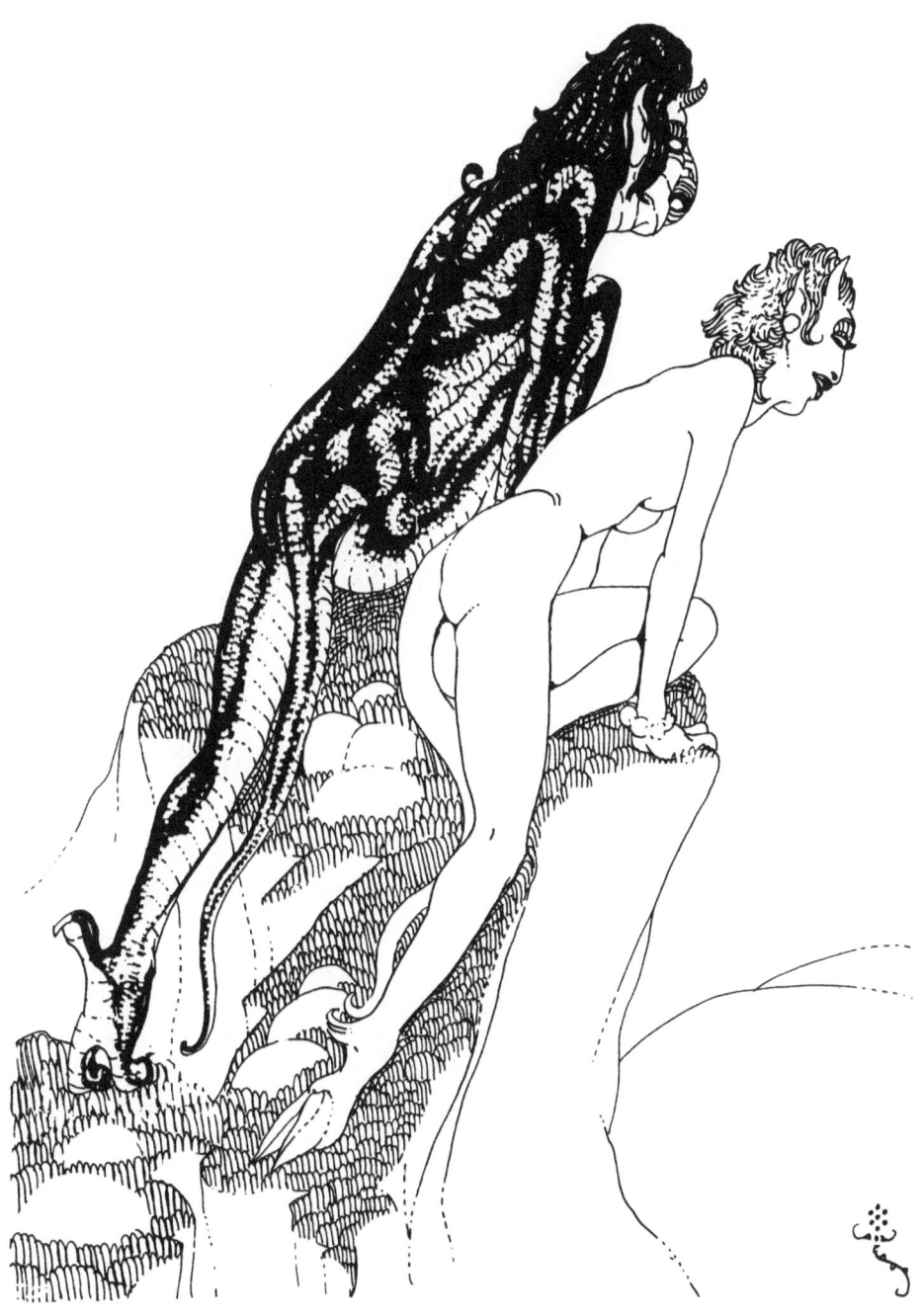

14. *And evil*

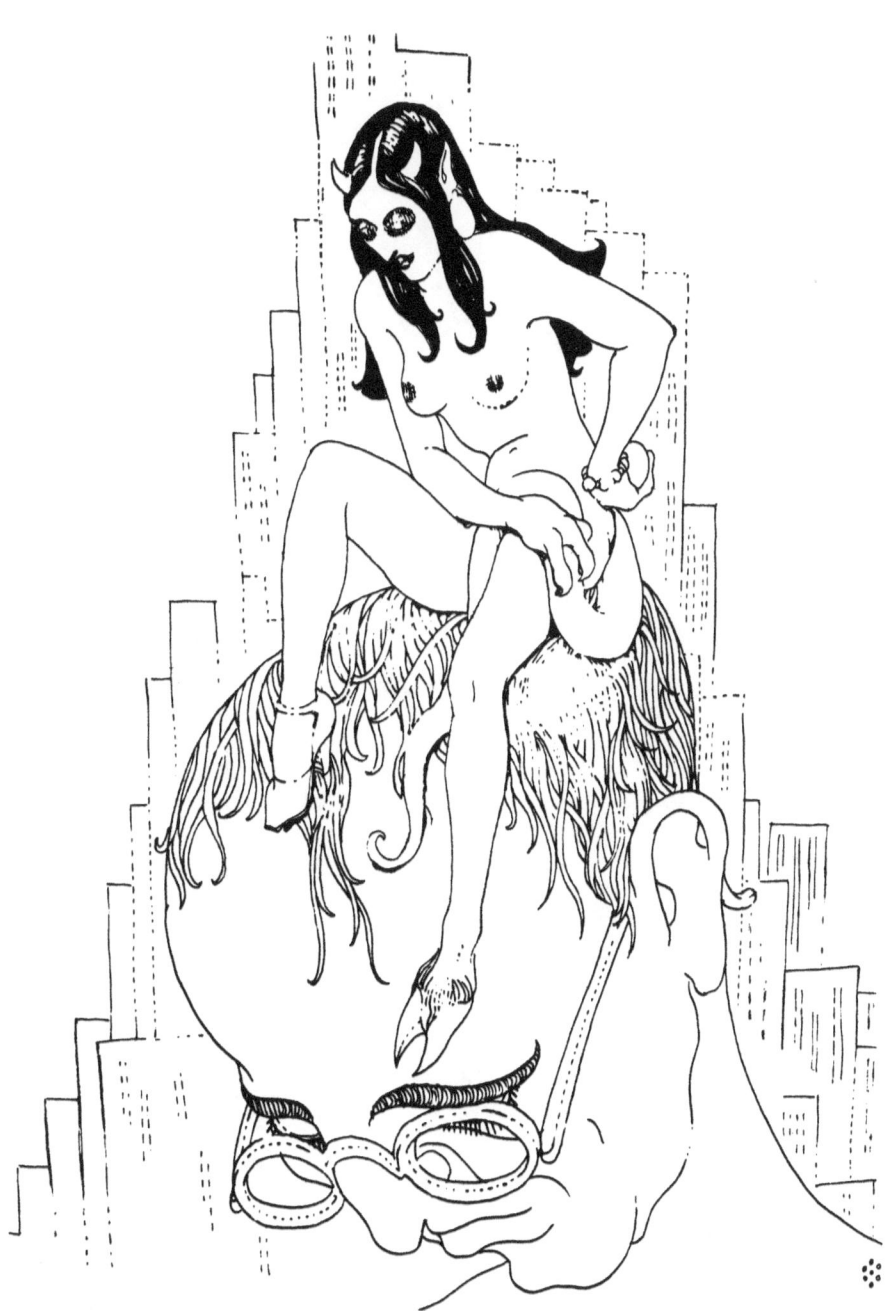

15. *And they thought of nought but lust*

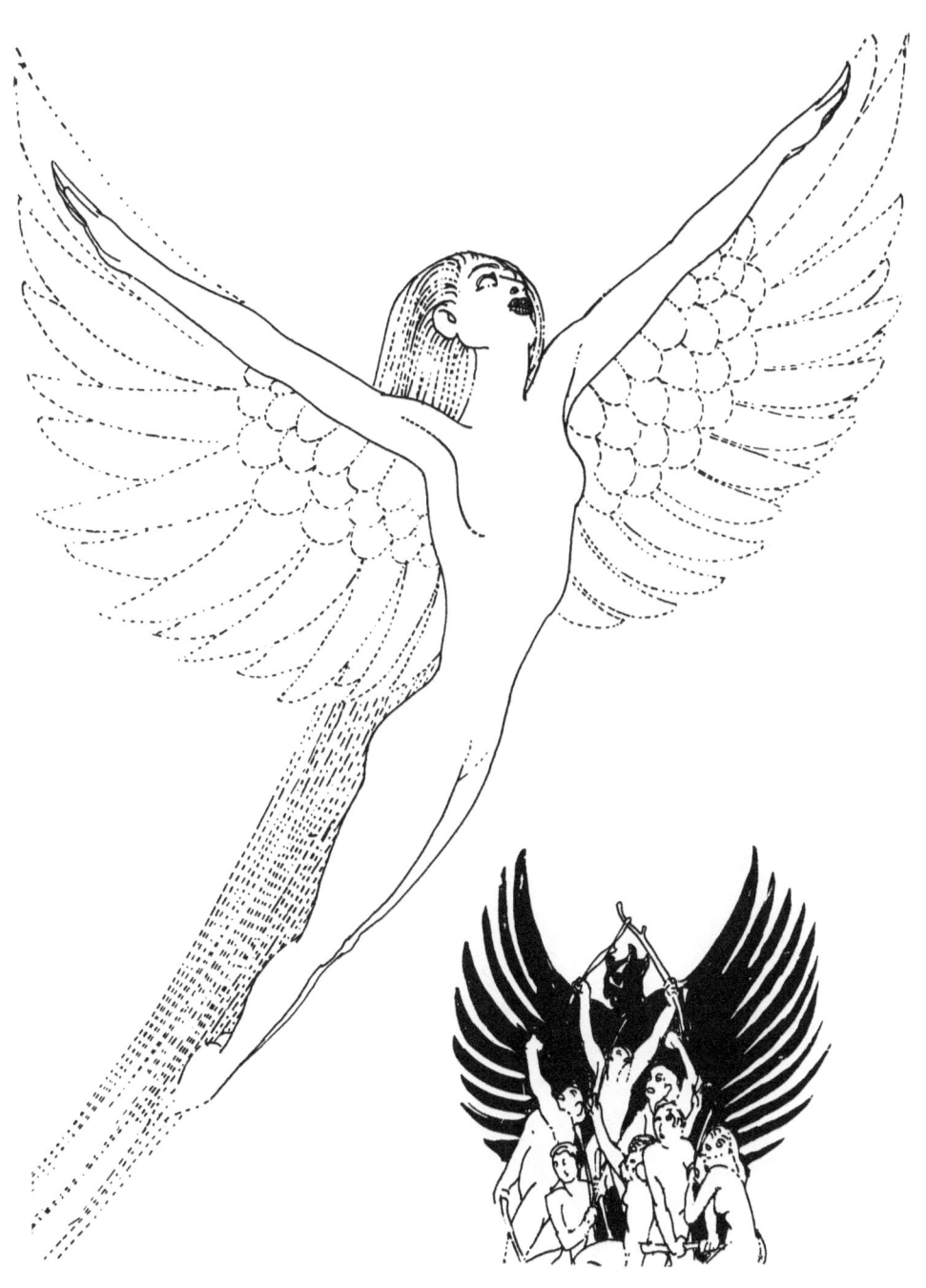

16. *Thus they chased love*

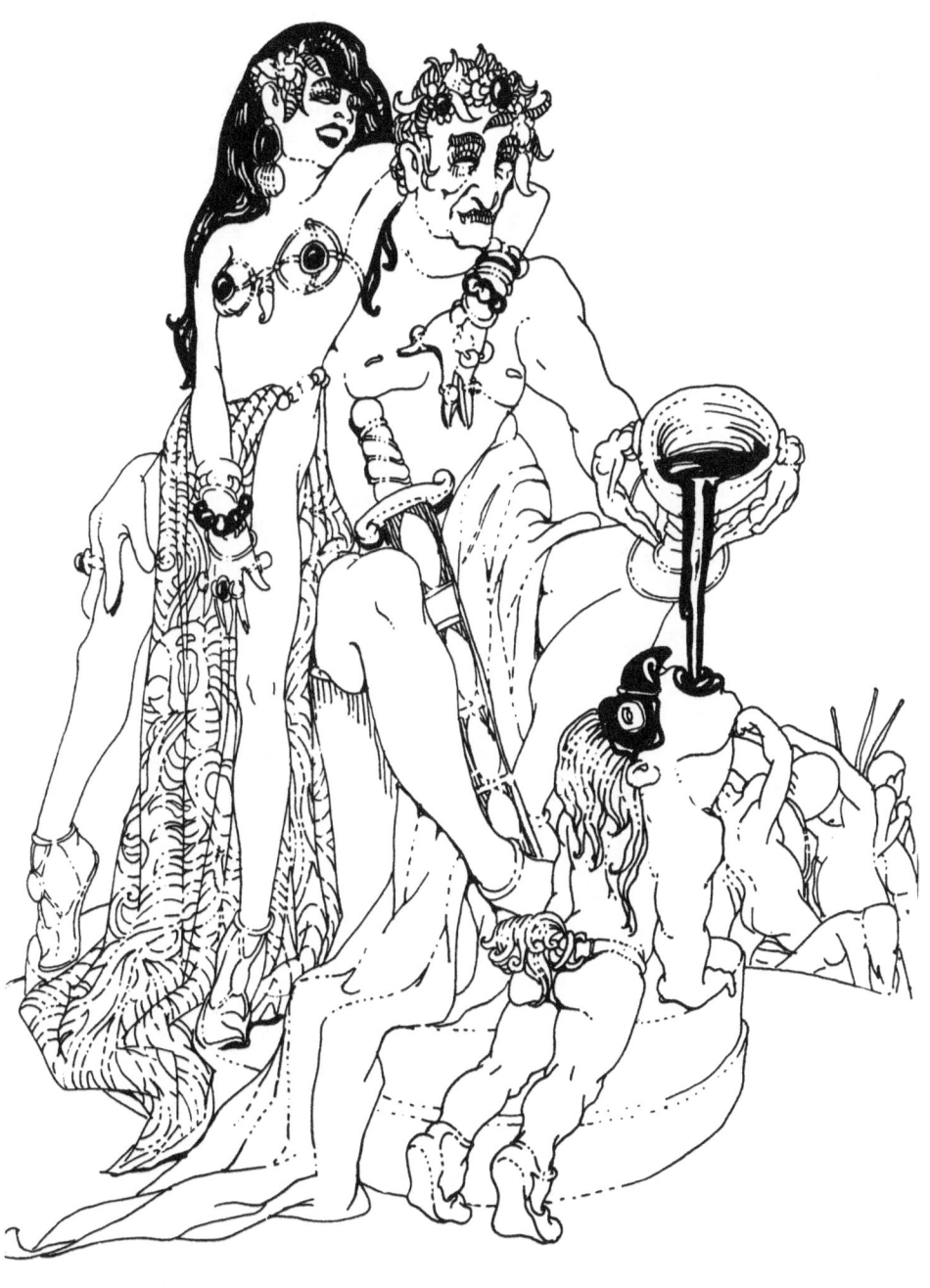

17. Laughter became scorn, life a combat

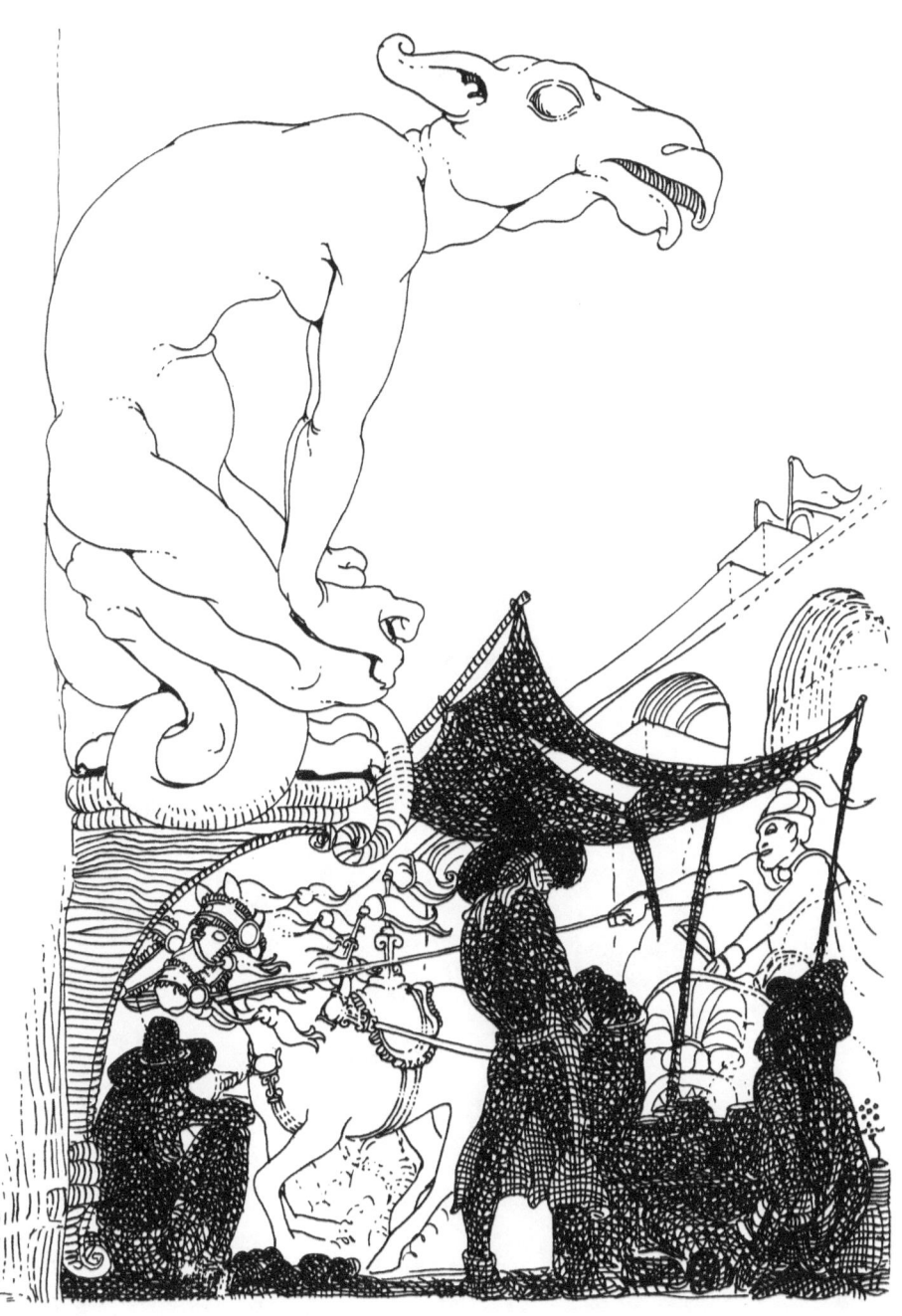

18. Groves gave way to market places

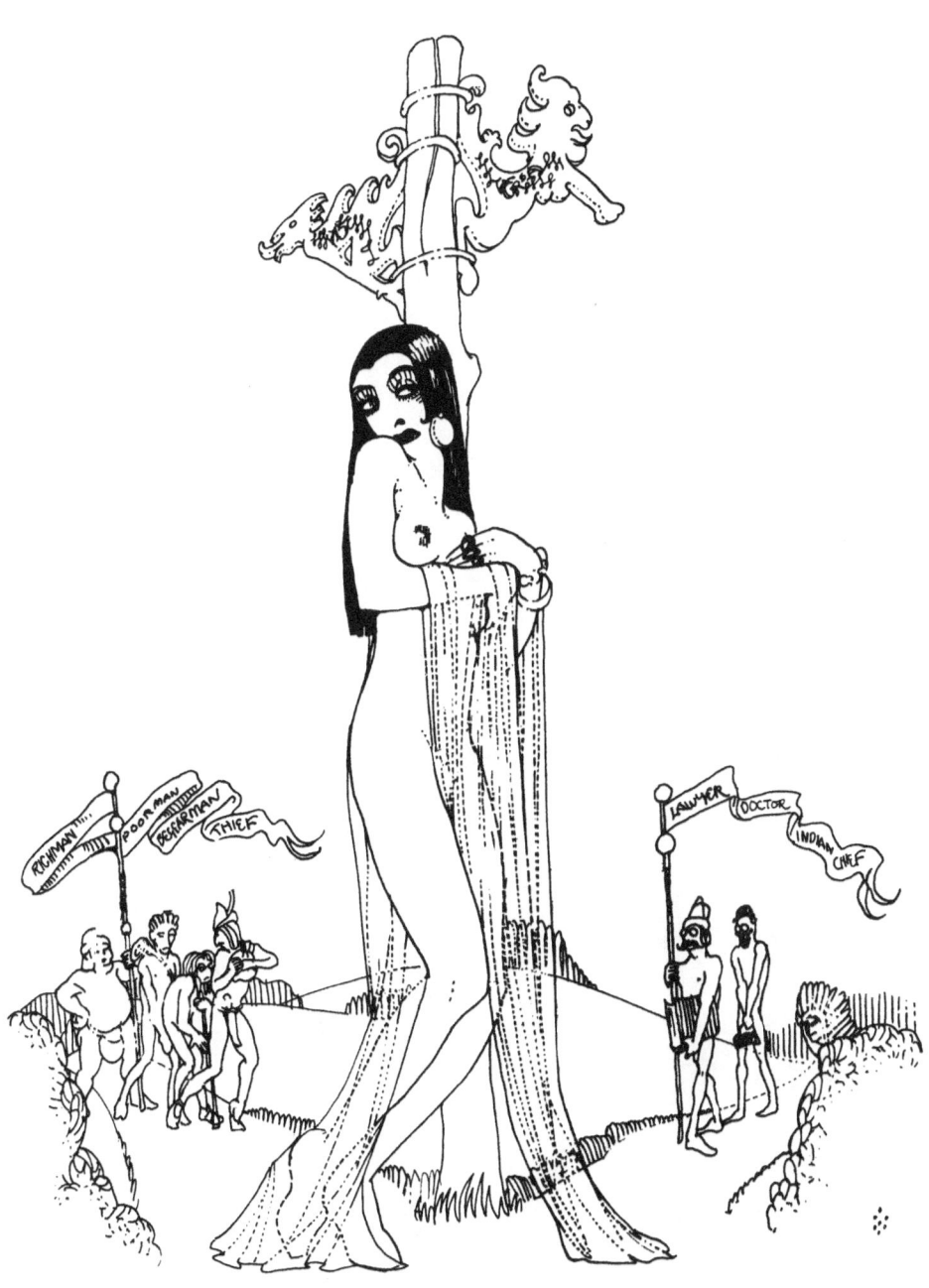

19. "Venus of the Crossways," sighed the realist

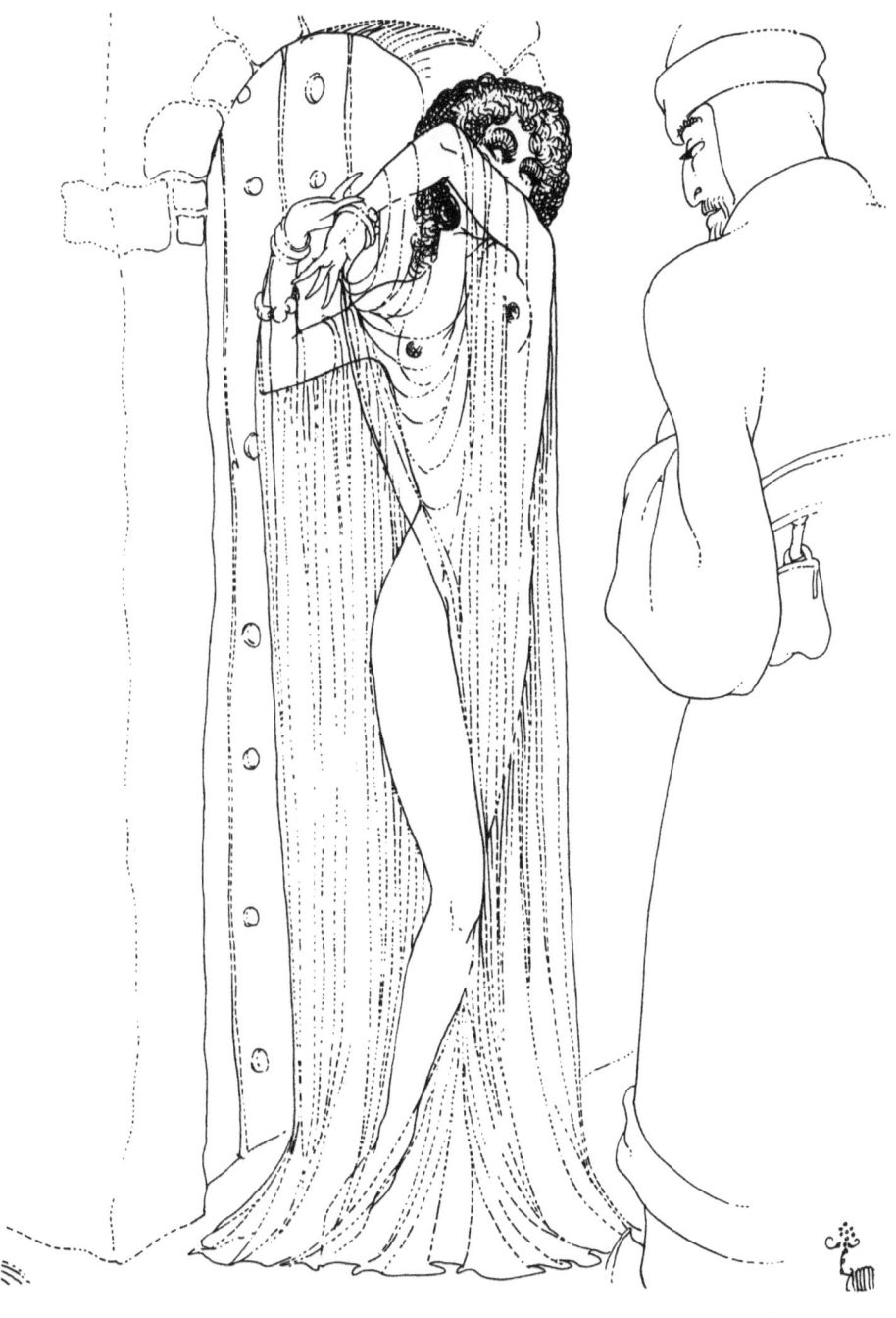

20. Love stood on the corner and bartered

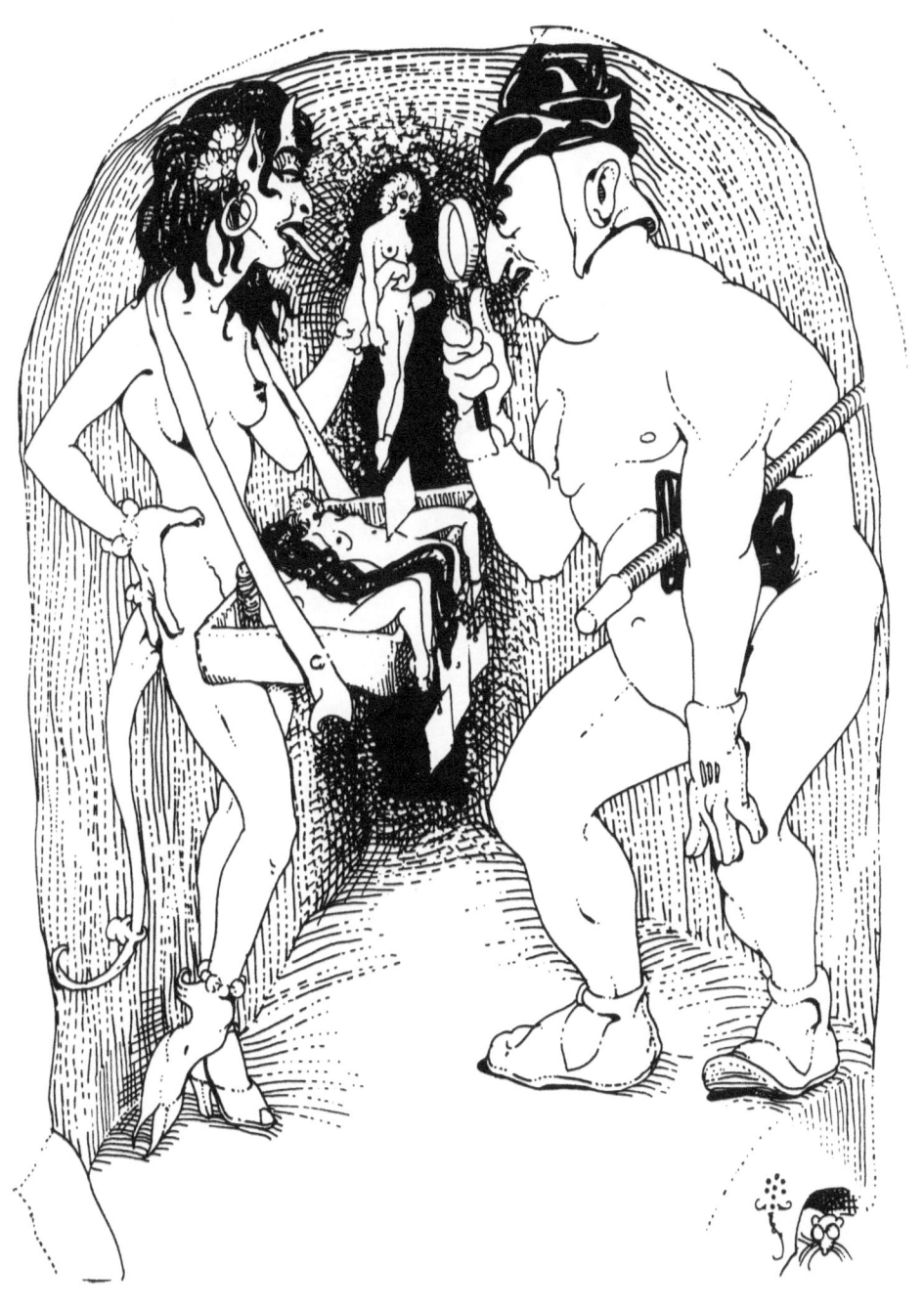

21. In secret places merchants offered new combinations

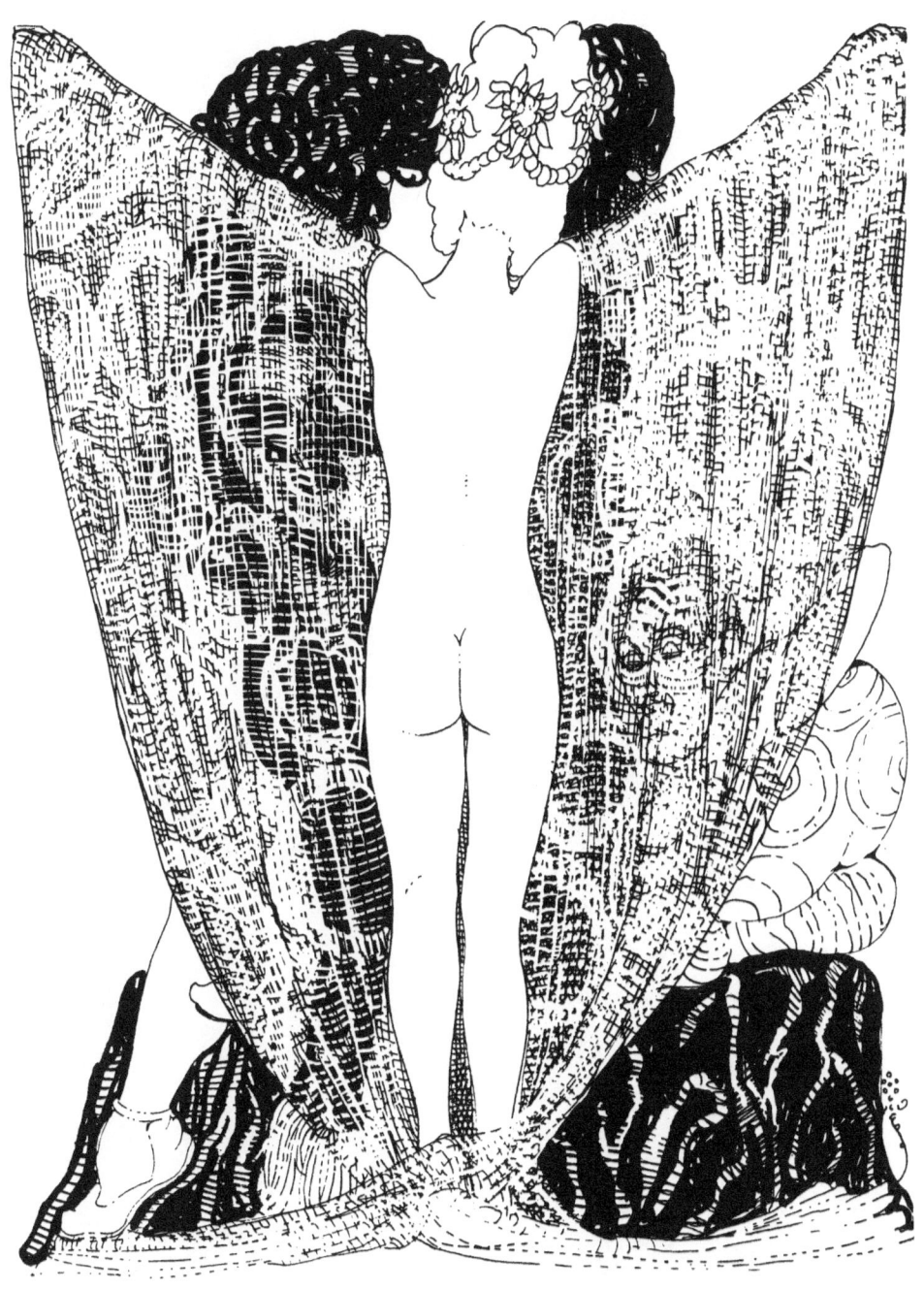

22. The cynical, cloyed with sophistication

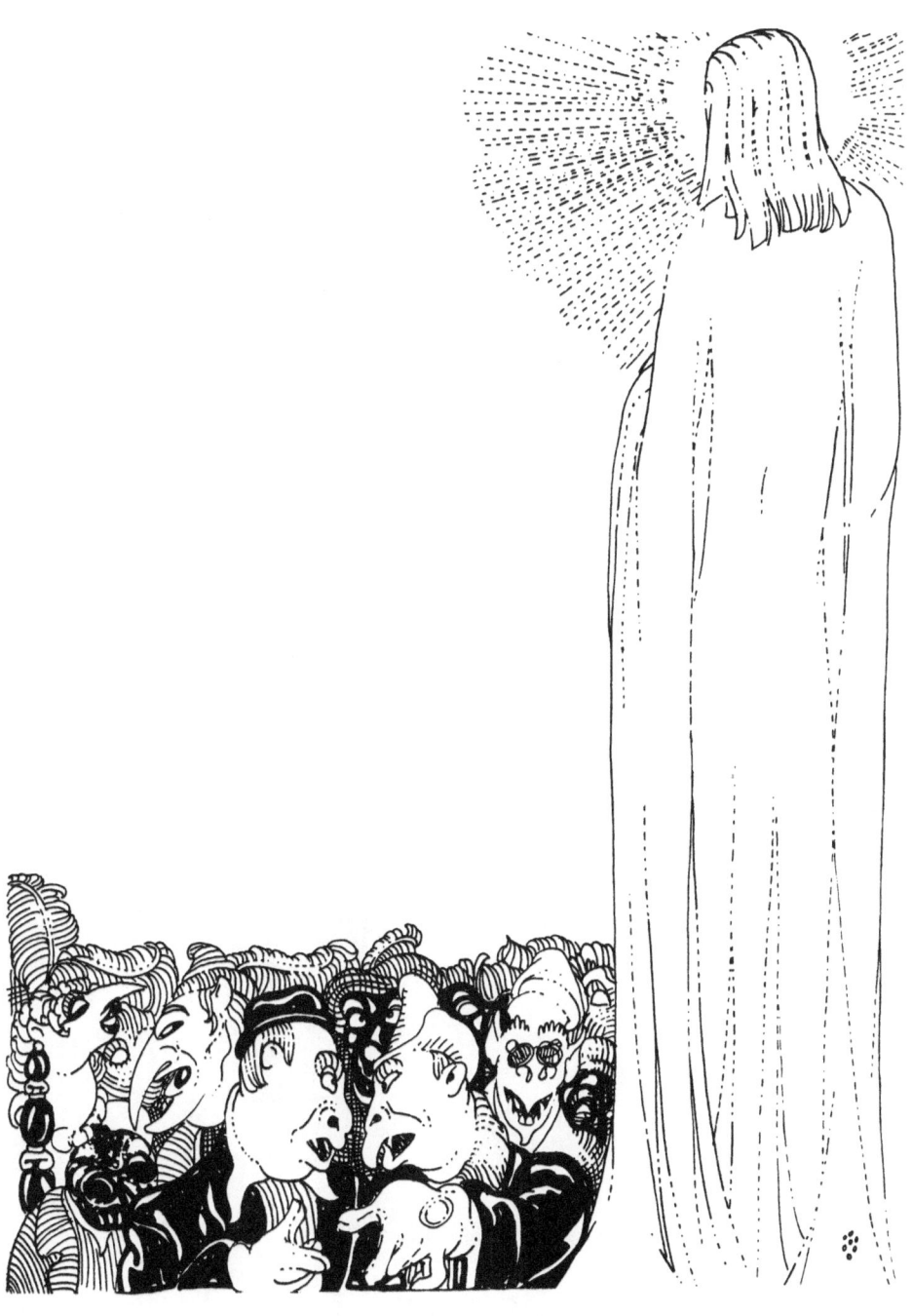

23. A stranger came and preached; LOVE

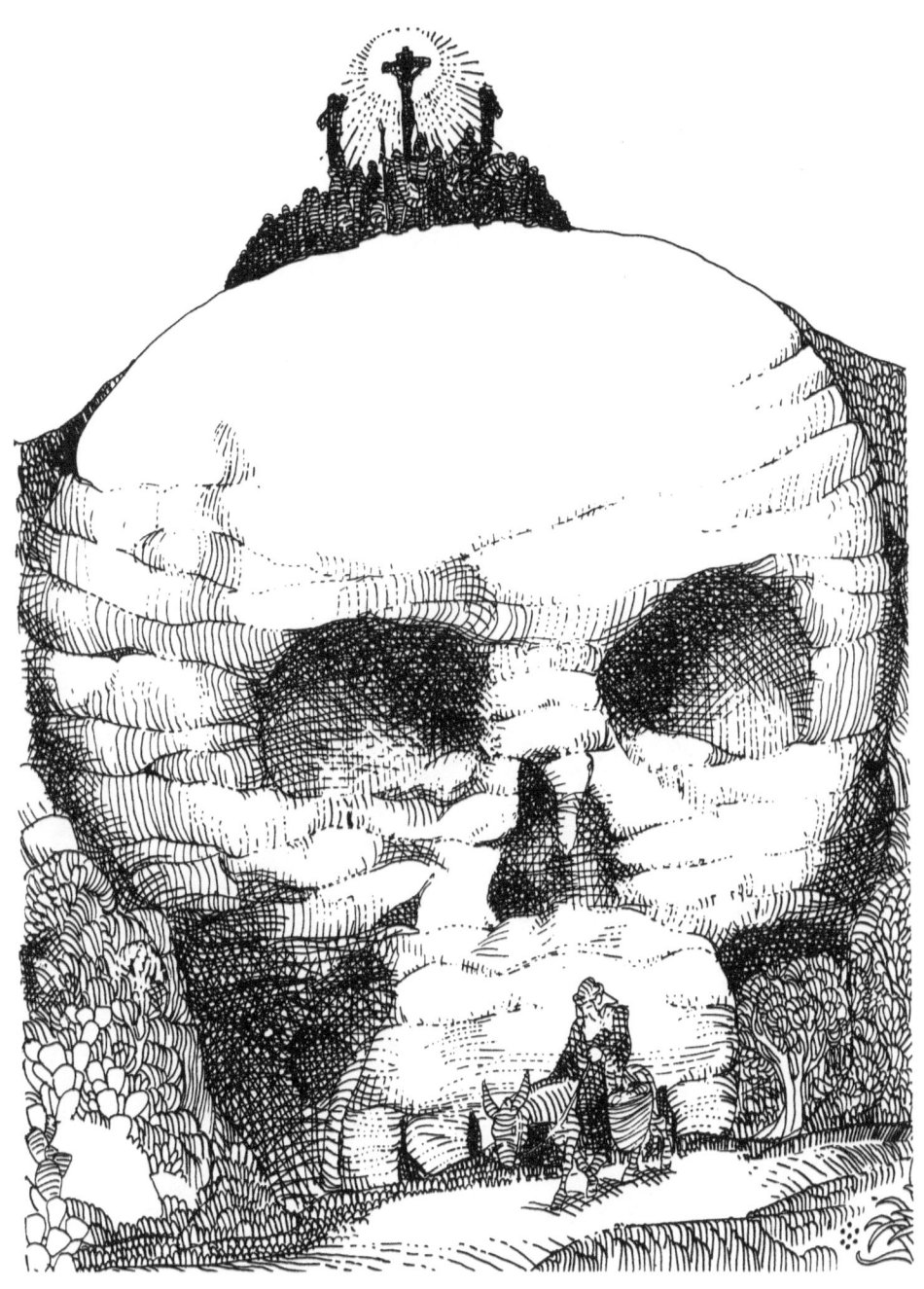

24. They mocked and crucified him

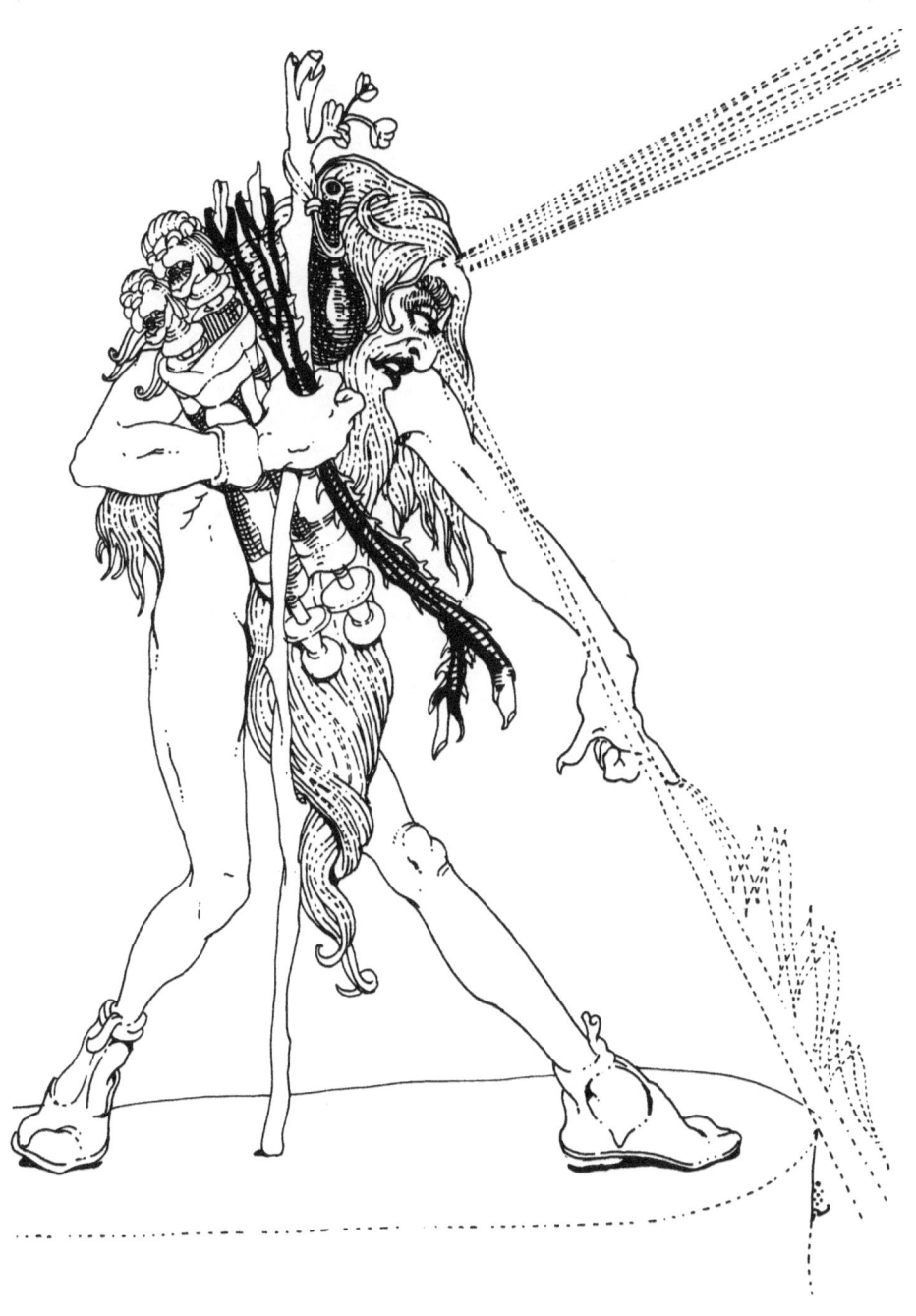

25. "Sin!" screamed the prophet

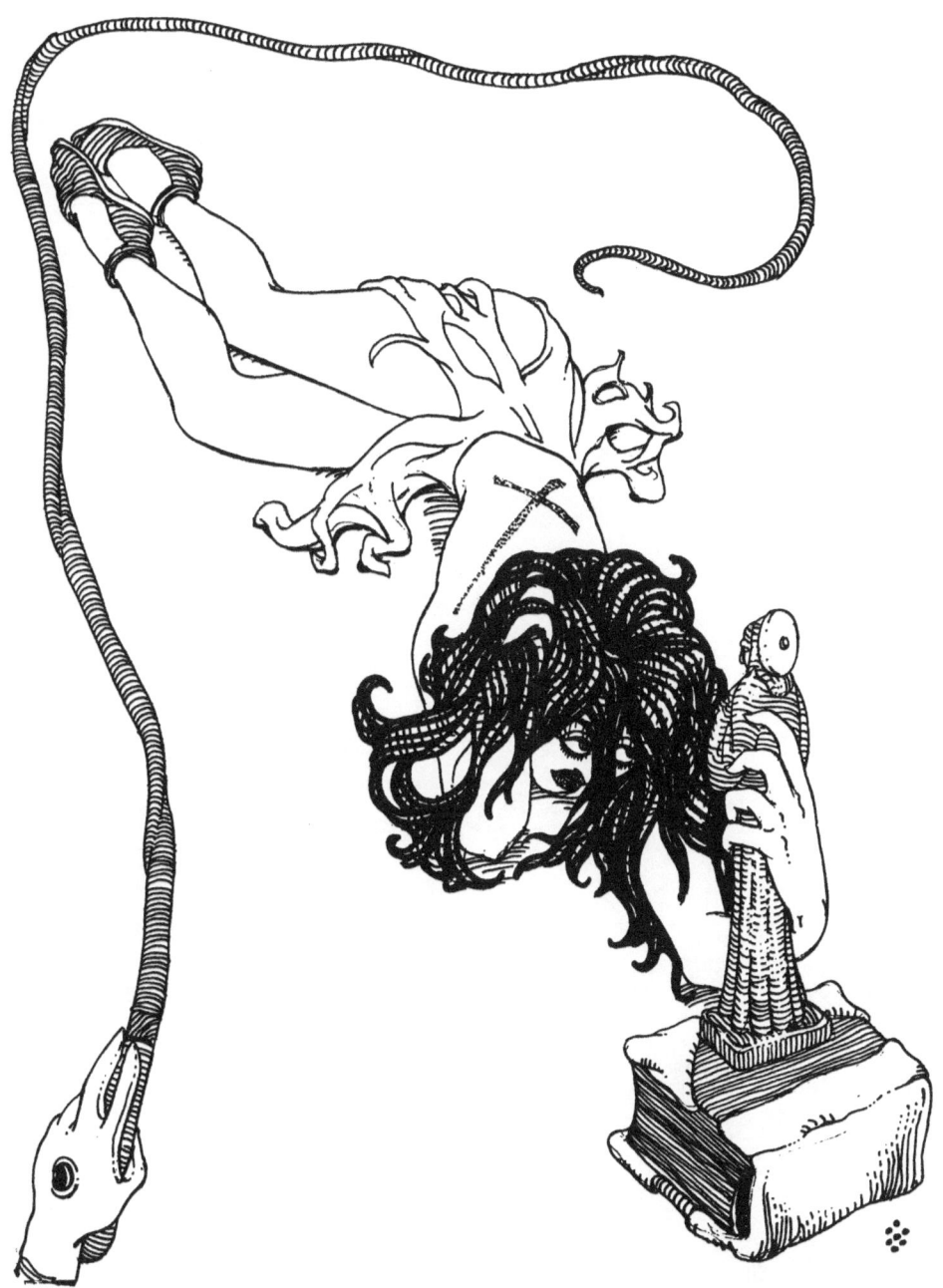

26. The saint writhed under the lash

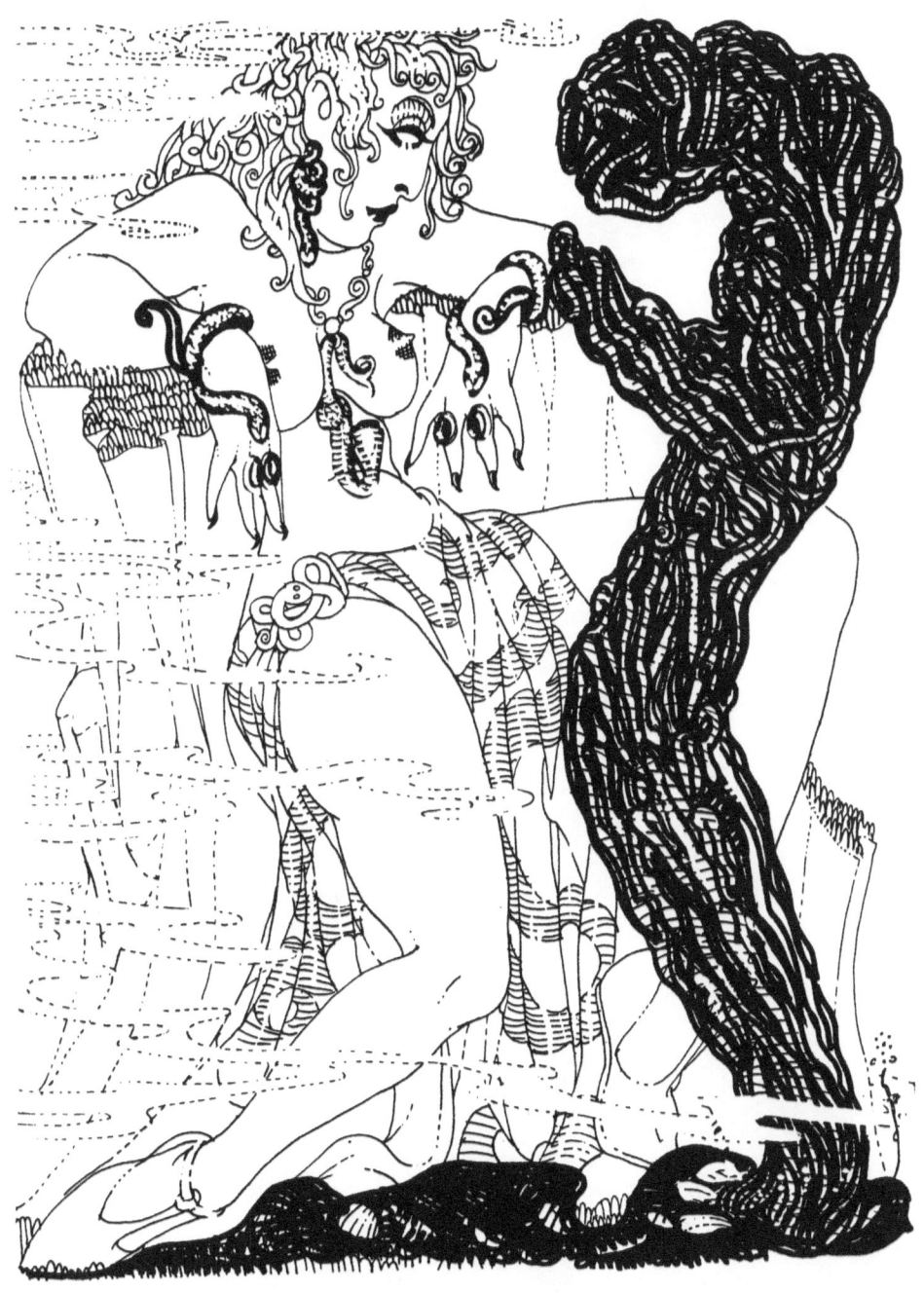

27. A black cloud rose out of hell

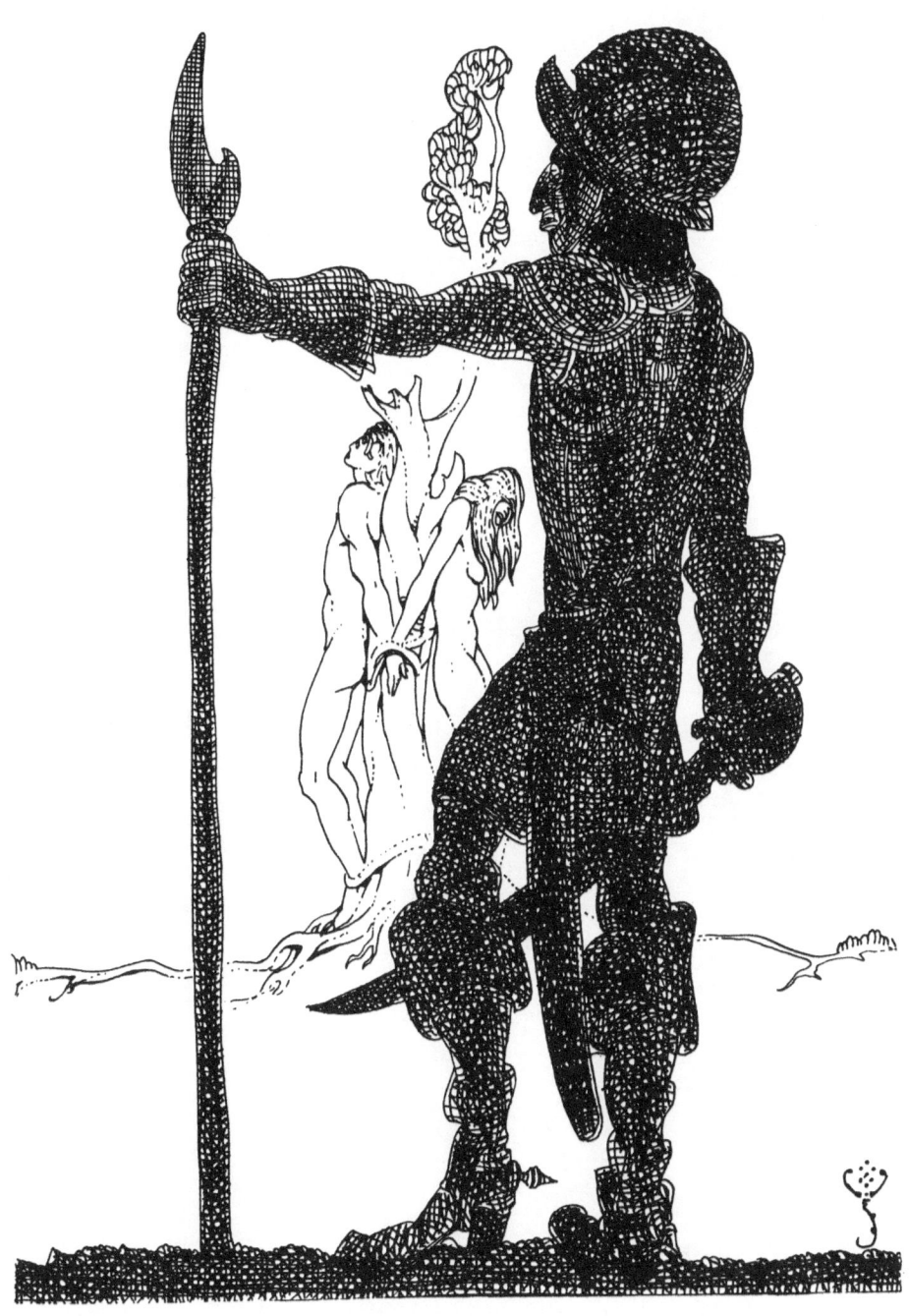

28. Saint and witch were methodically suppressed

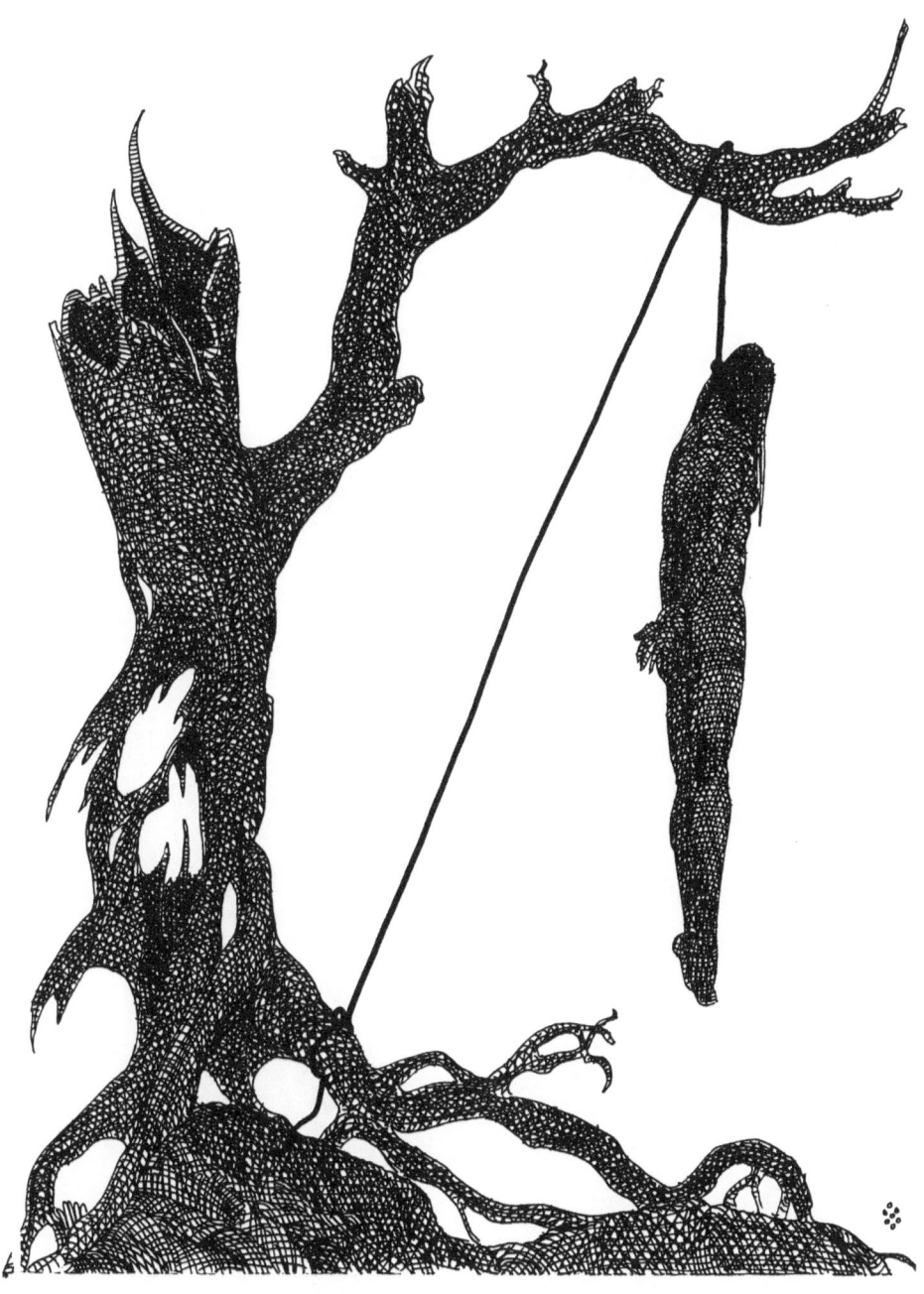

29. "Duty," they said as they hanged the witch

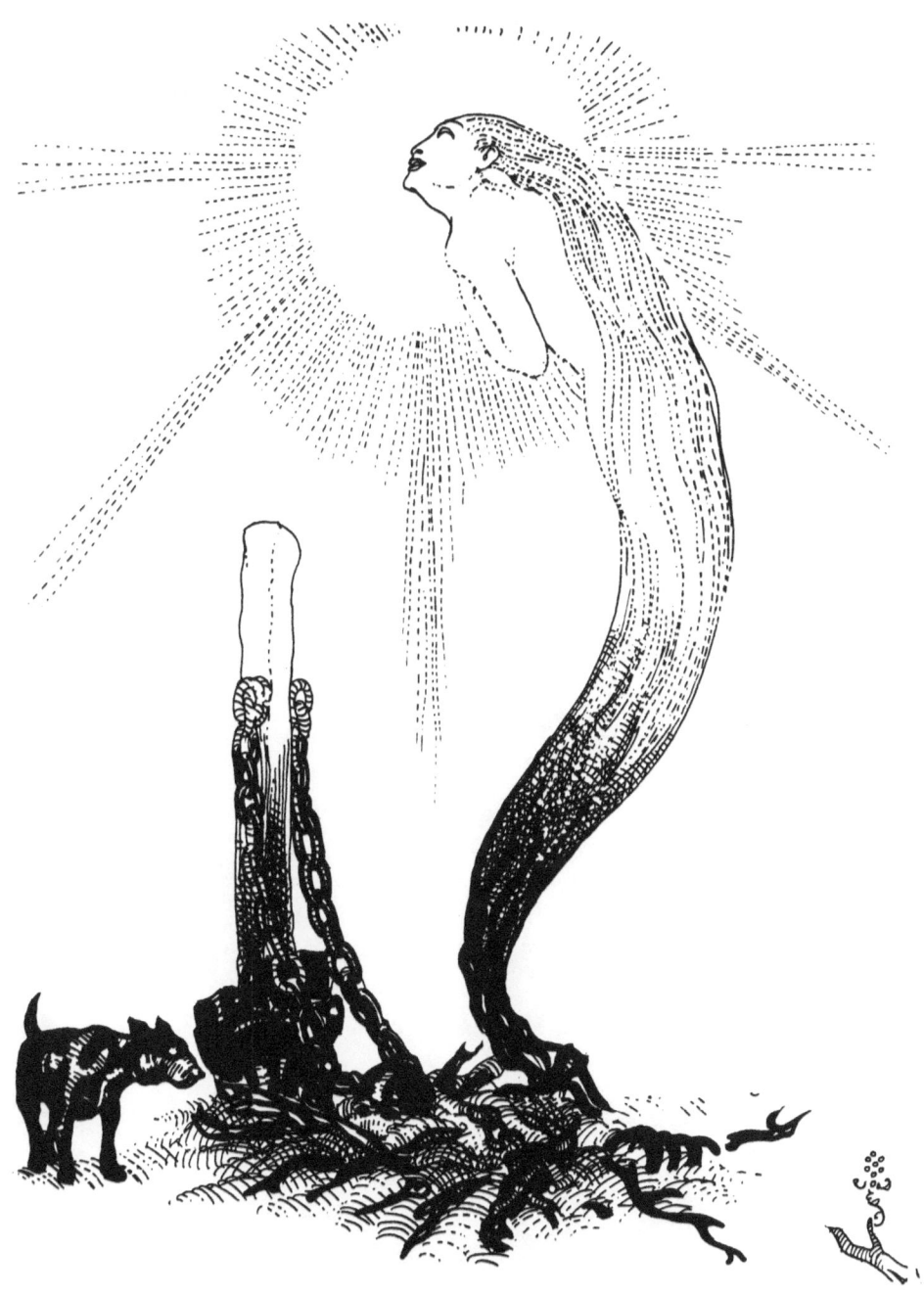

30. Burned the saint

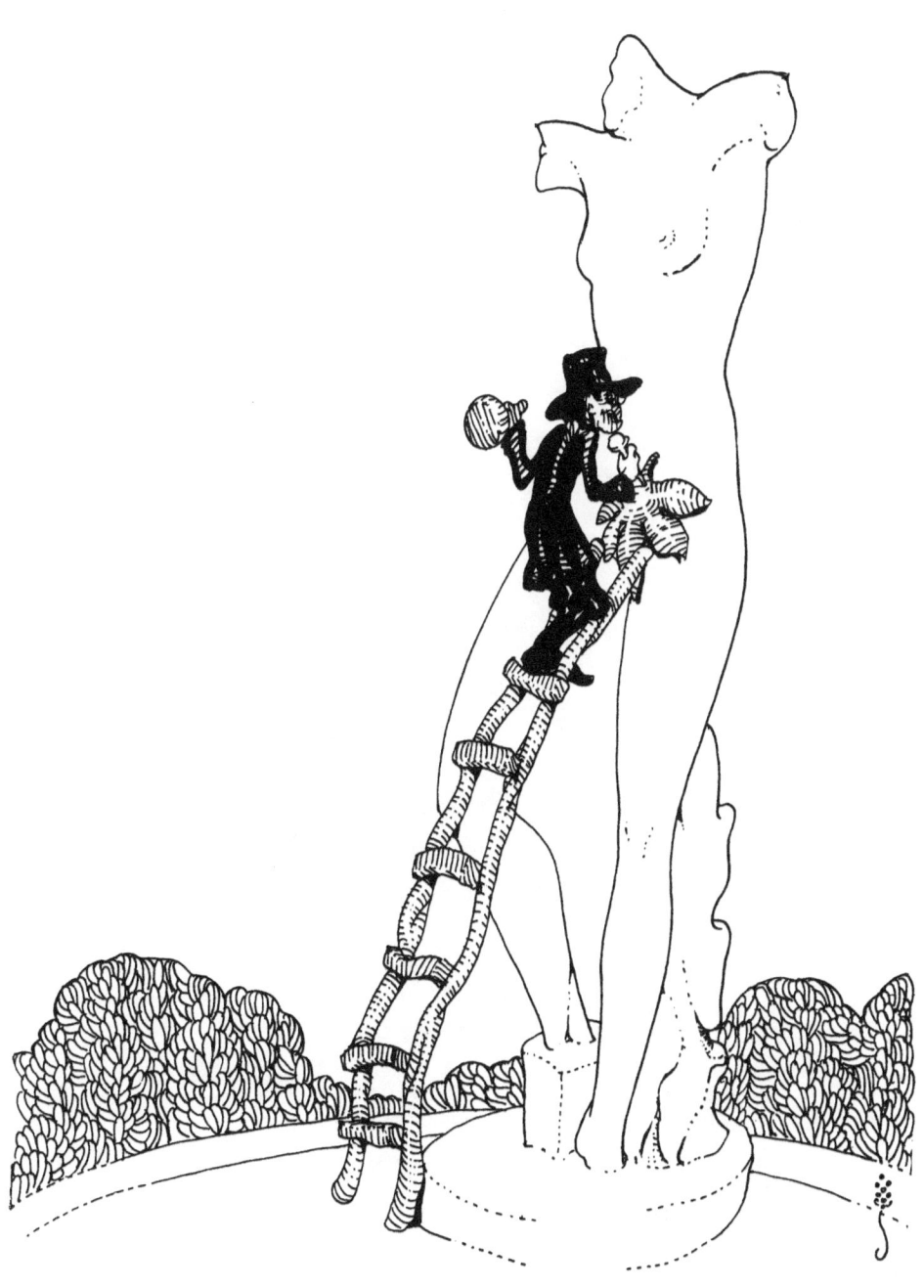

31. And put aprons on antique statues

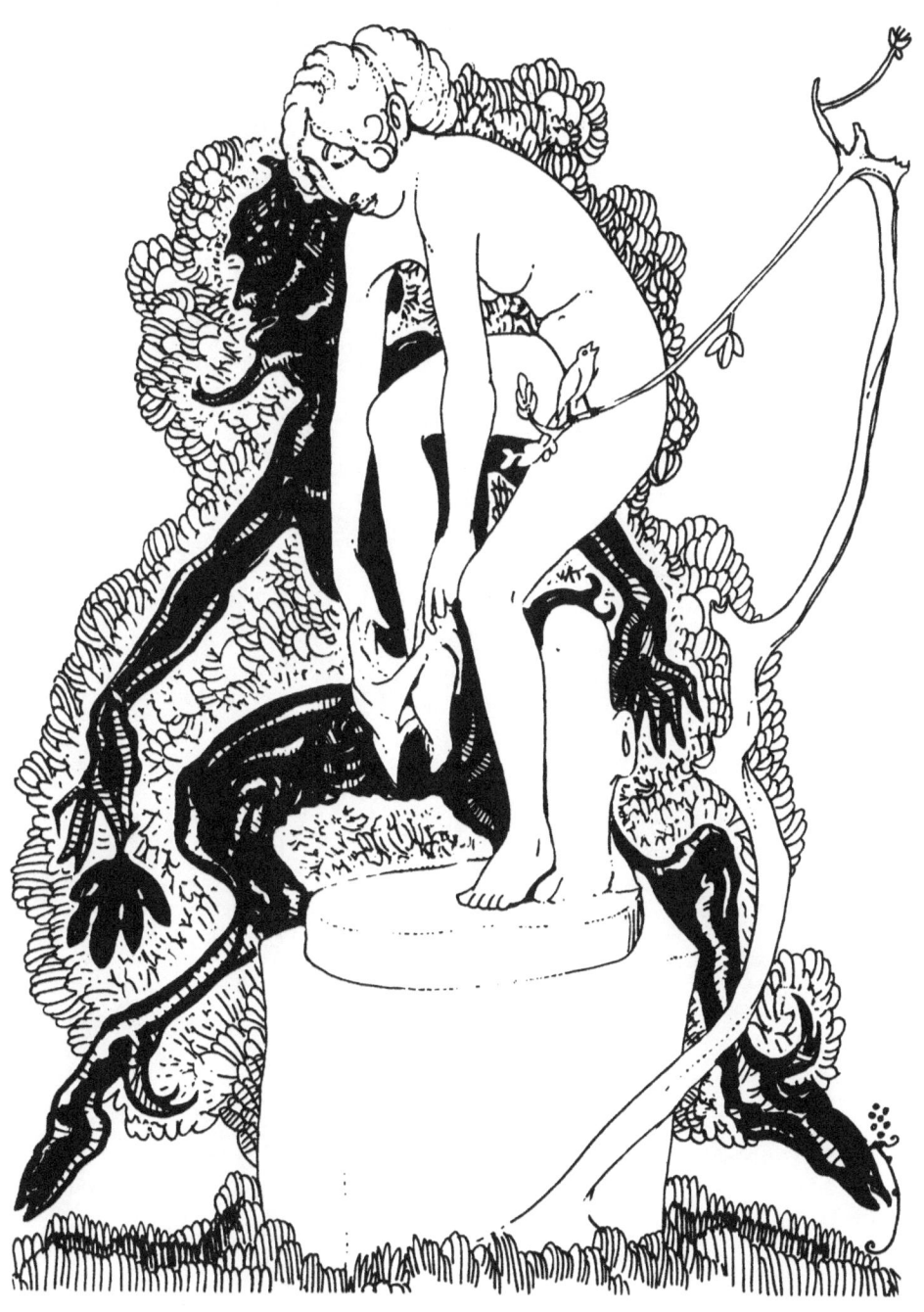

32. The aprons slipped

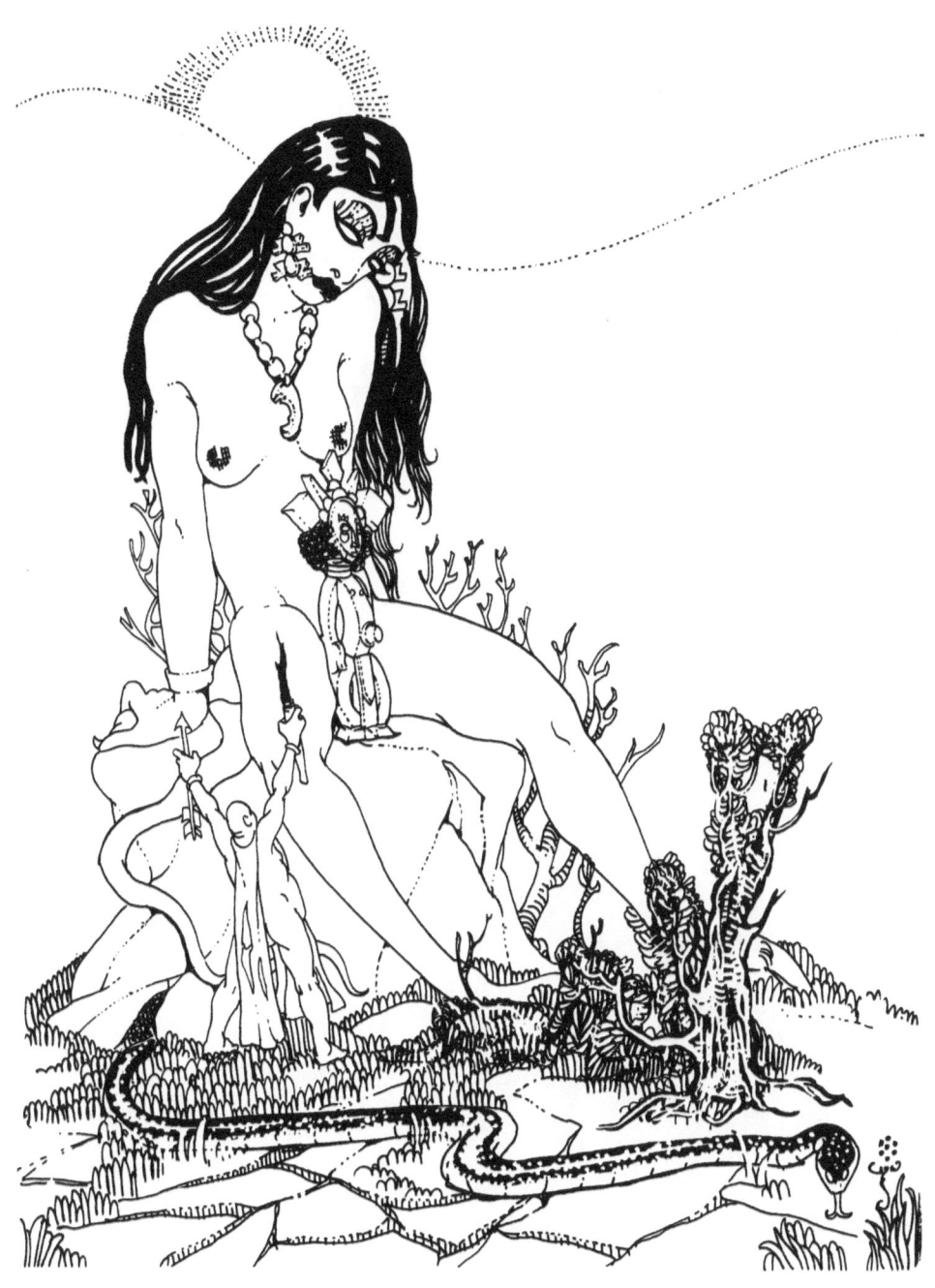

33. The fervor of saintliness had long been quenched

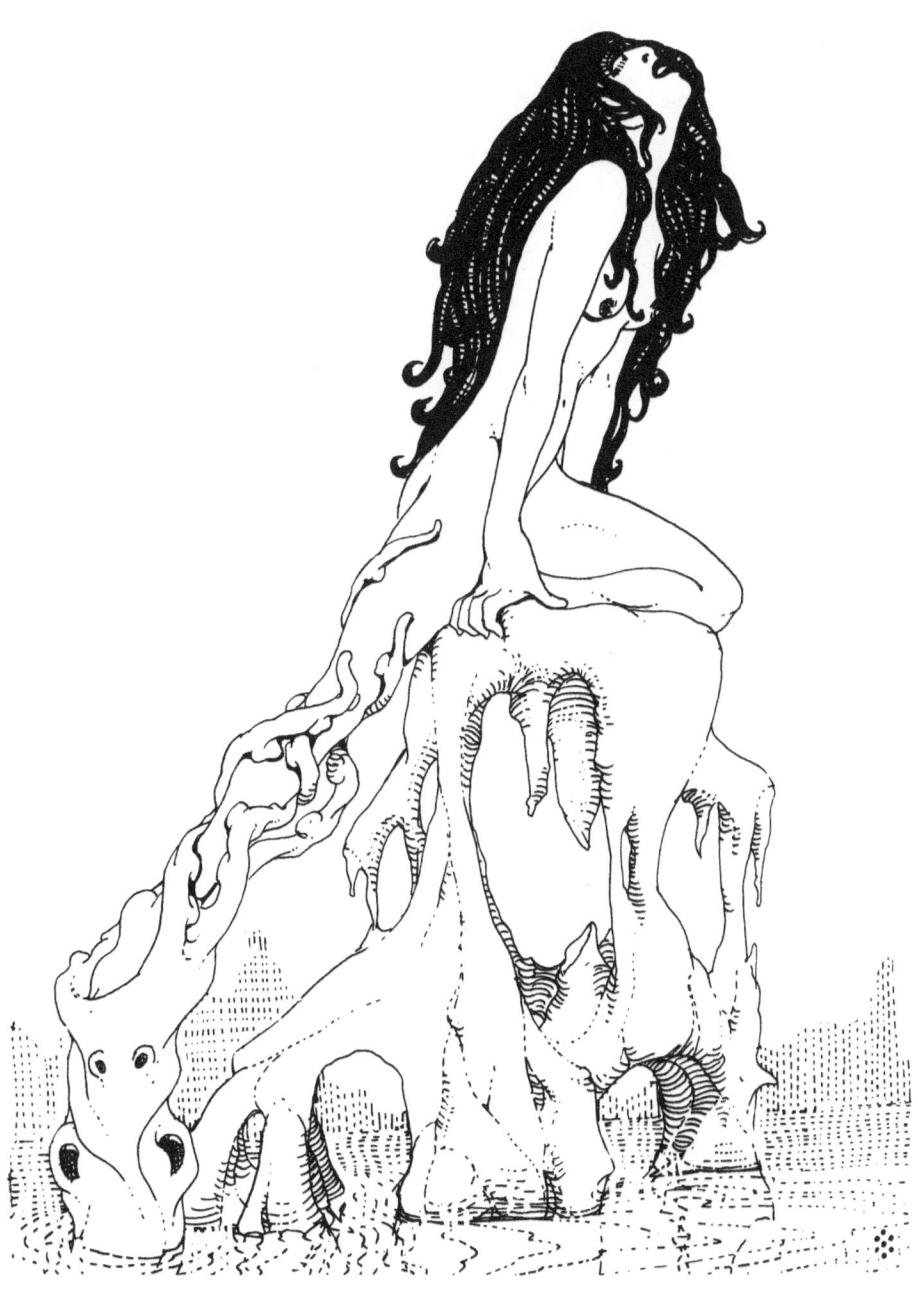

34. Sourness sought alkalinity

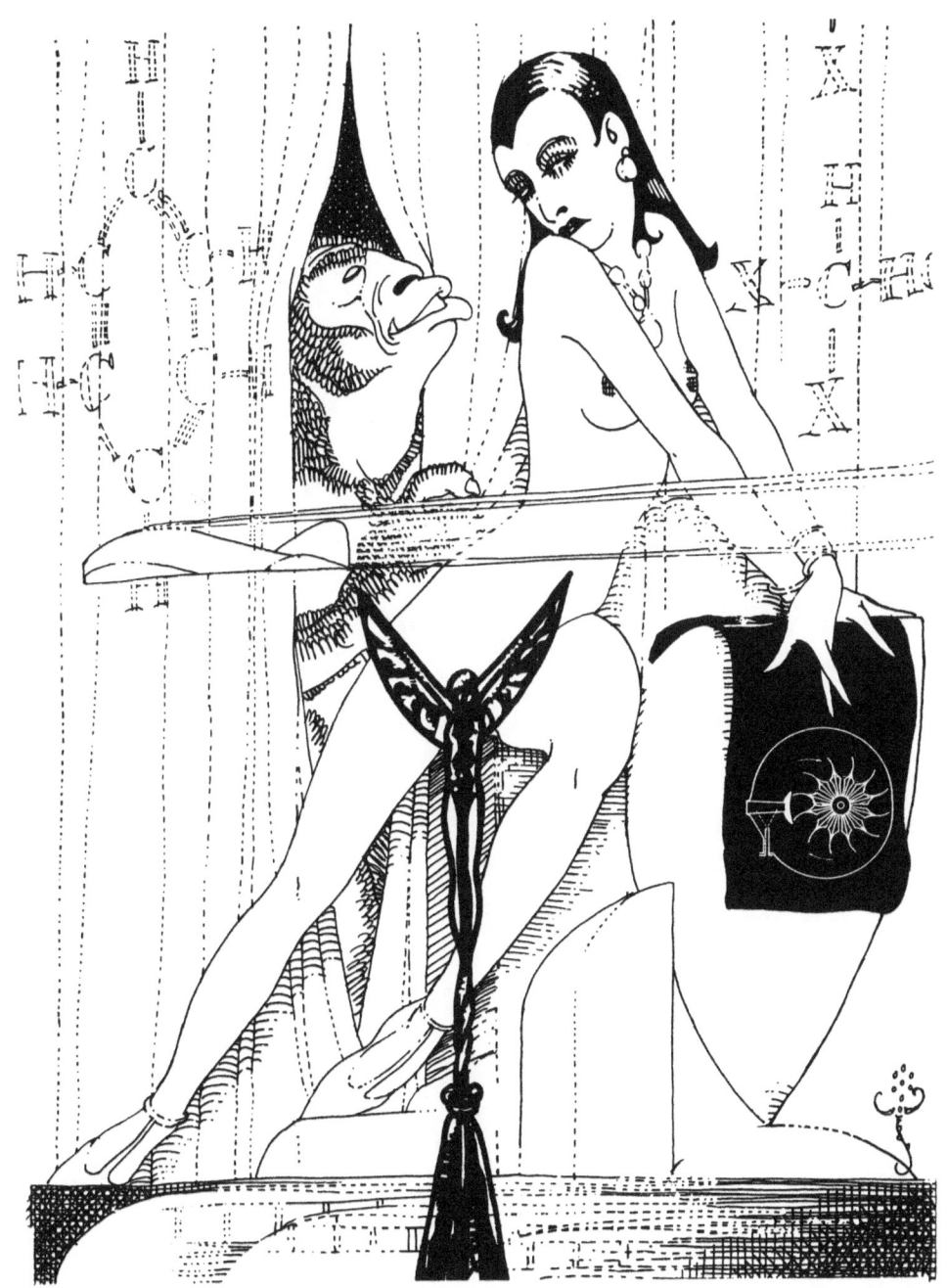

35. A streamlined era

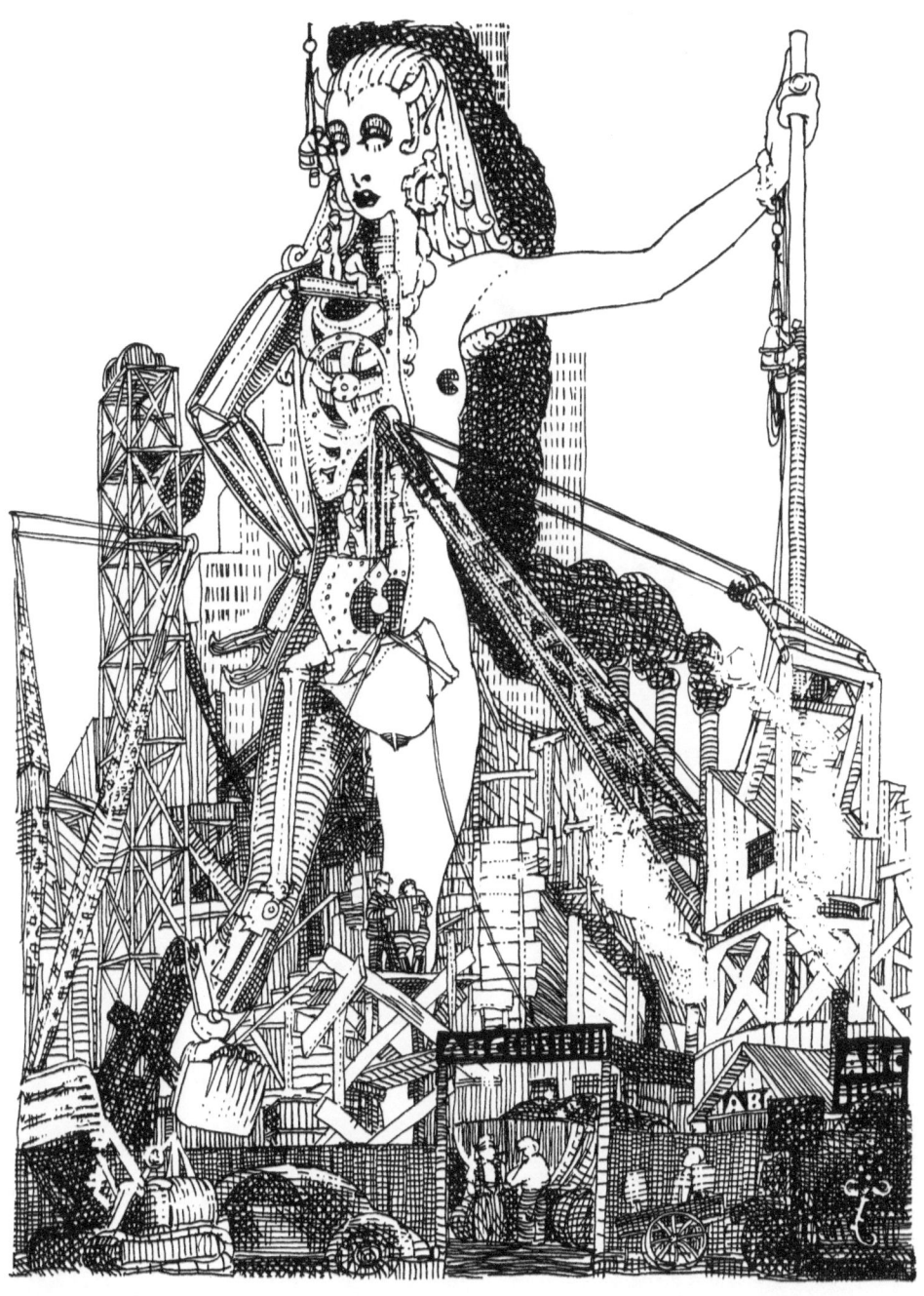

36. Created a diety in its own image

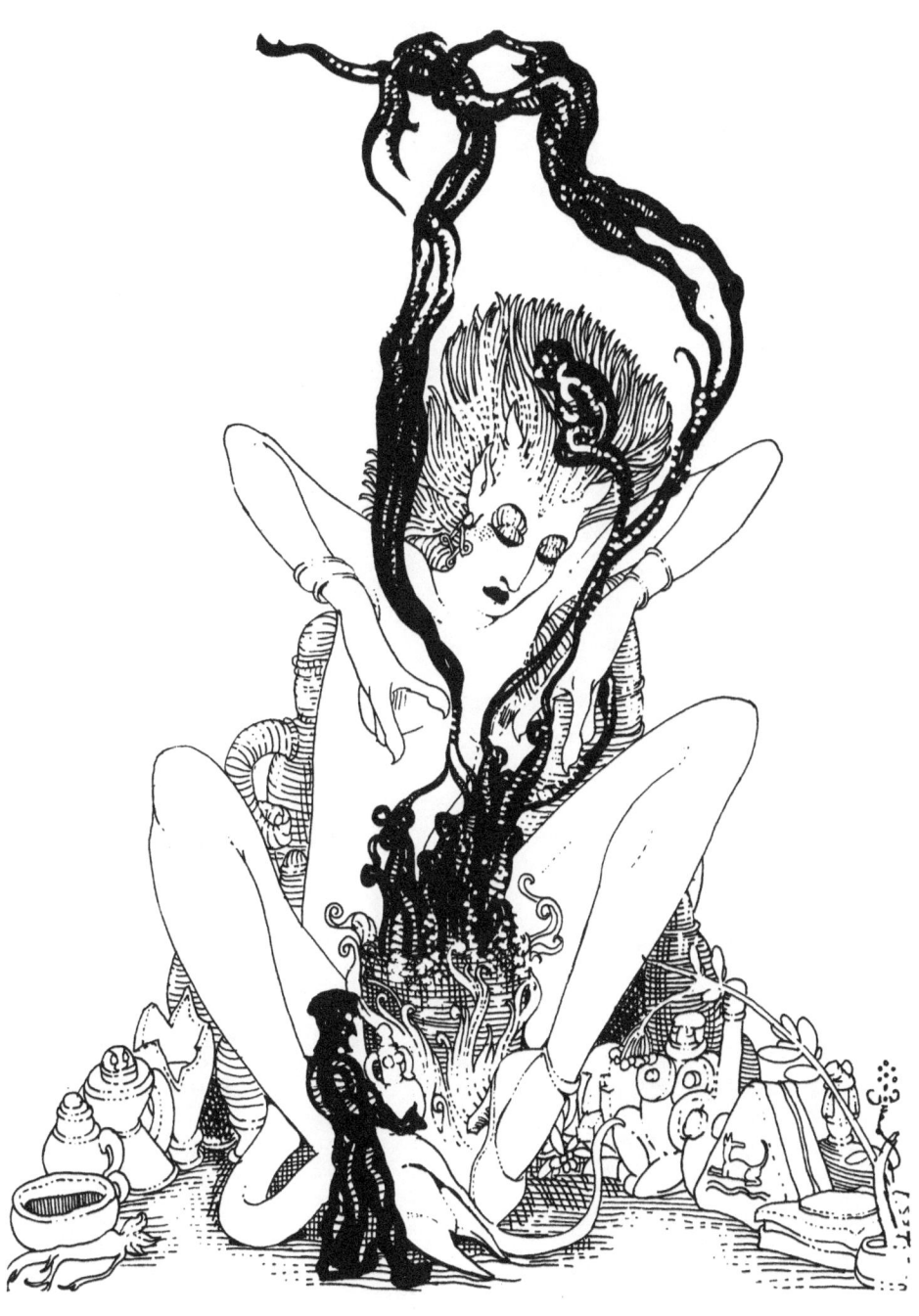

37. She is an irreverent enchantress

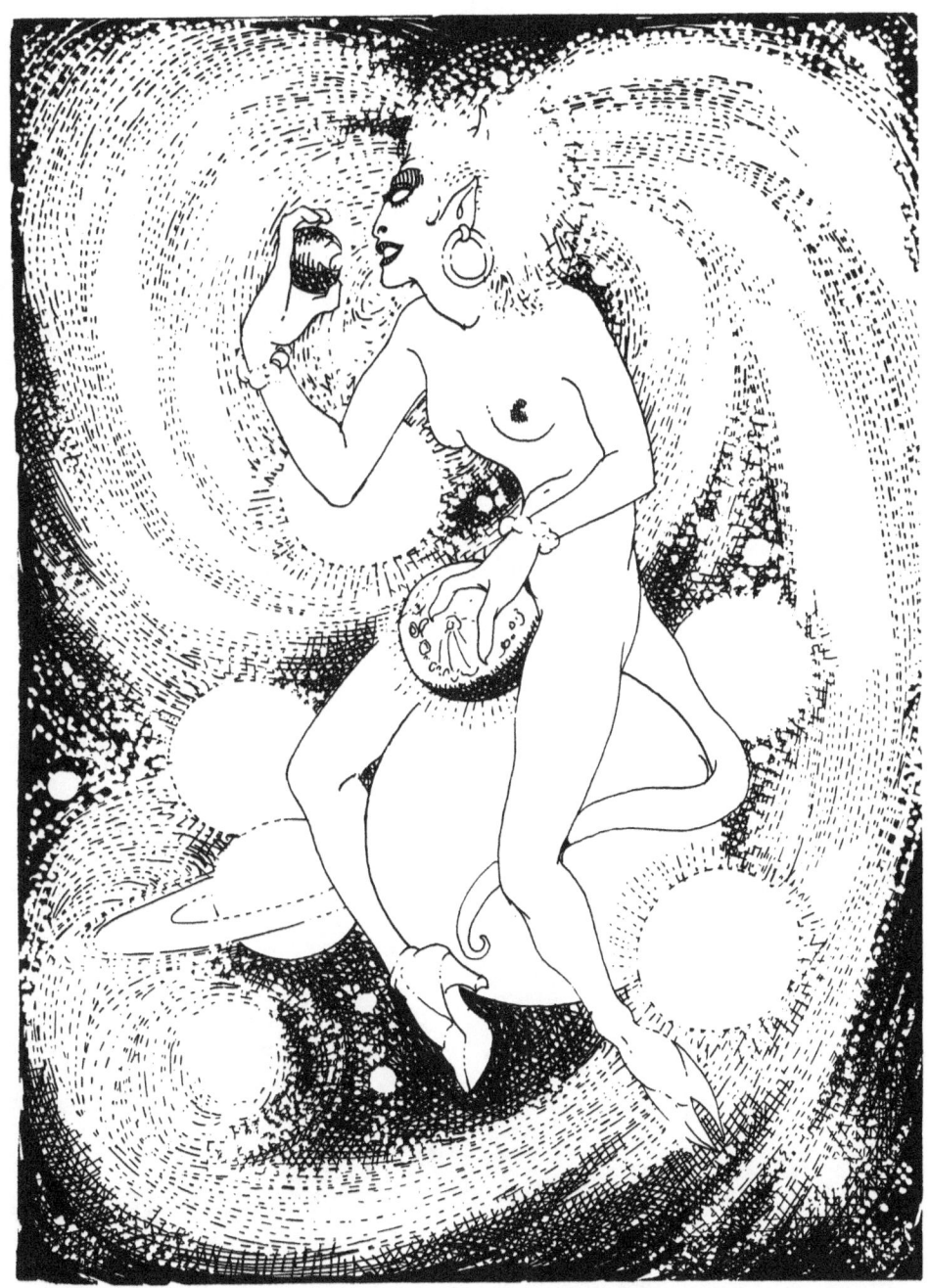

38. An uncanny wisdom, of the world and other worlds

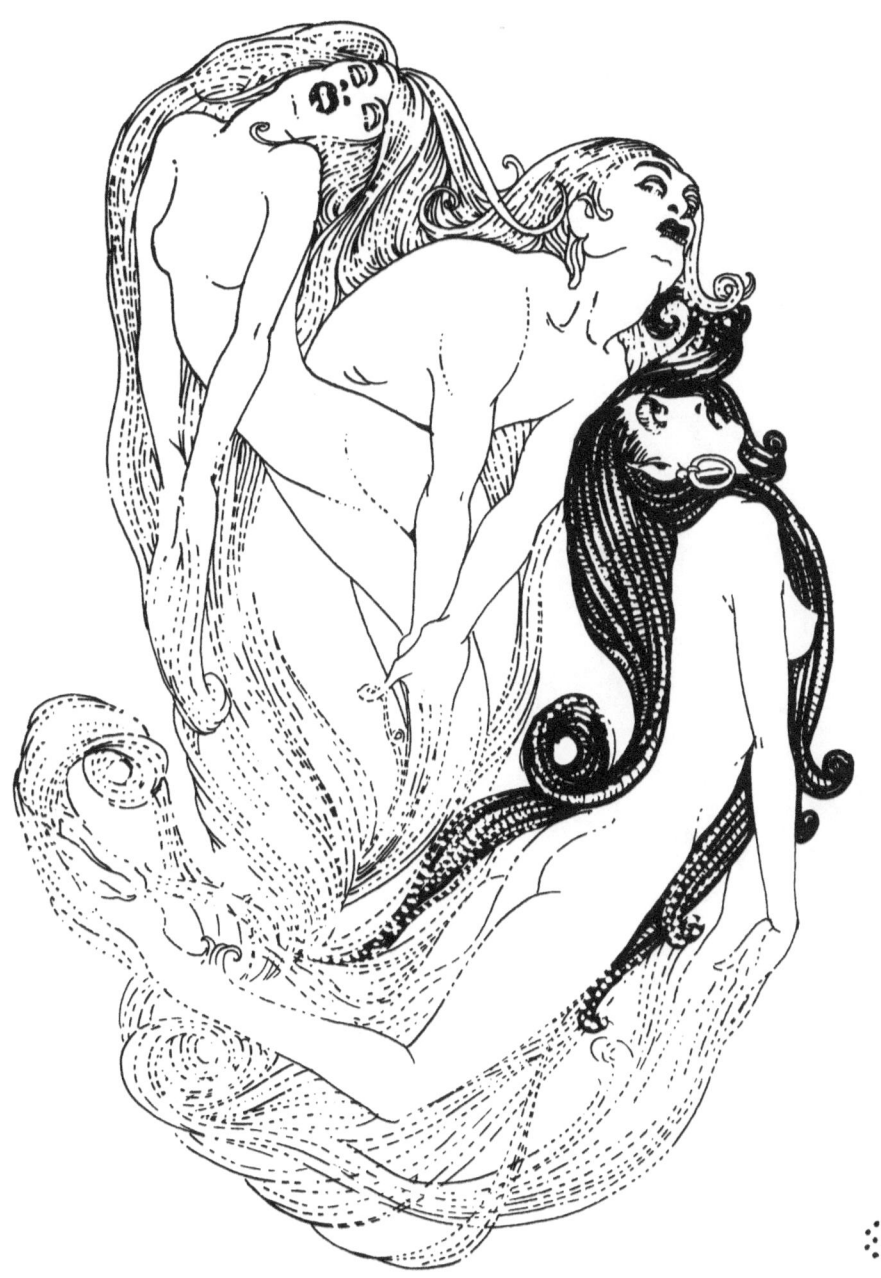

39.   Hers is the realm where all things touch

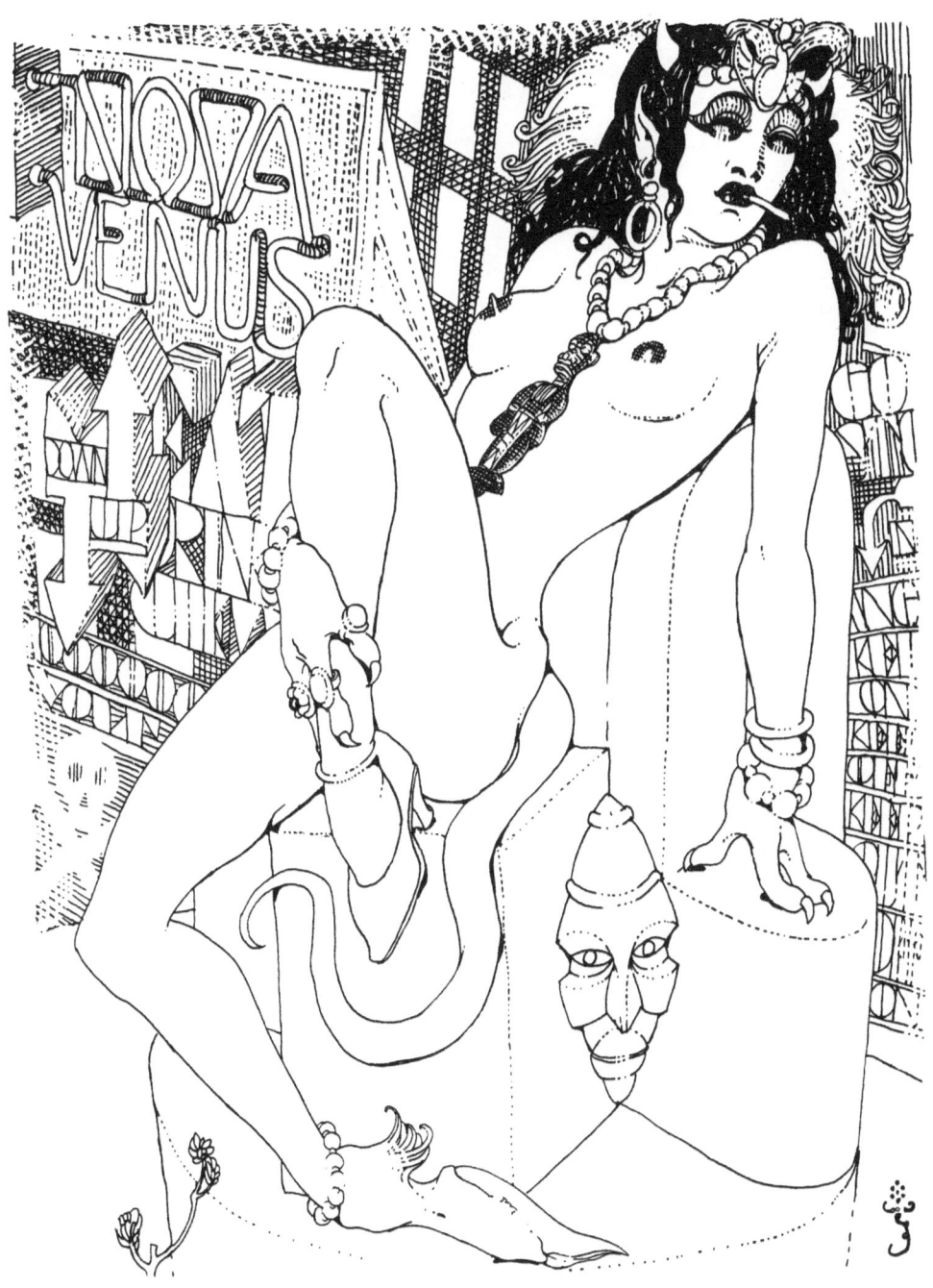

40. She is Nova Venus

The Outlandish Art Of Mahlon Blaine

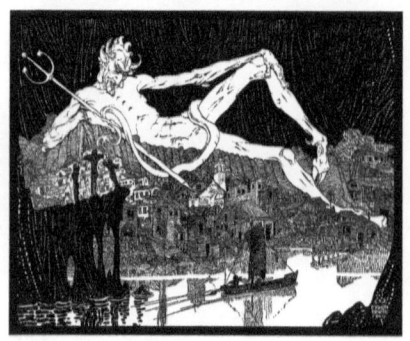

Edited by Brian J. Hunt

In 1923 Mahlon Blaine burst upon the art scene with striking works of imagination and vision. Within a short time his work was published in everything ranging from children's books and mainstream magazines to erotic portfolios. The body of work he produced between 1926 and 1930 was nothing short of phenomenal but after 1931 his output became increasingly sporadic. Sadly like so many artists before him who have given us so much, Blaine died penniless and mostly forgotten in January of 1969. This volume samples Mahlon Blaine's unique artistic visions, from his grand emergence in the roaring 20's through his declining years in the swinging 60's.

The Outlandish Art of Mahlon Blaine
http://www.mahlonblaine.com

"This is an overdue recognition of Blaine's fine eye for details in his drawings. You have presented his work in chronological order, which shows his development over the years, giving us an insight into his imaginative art. I am happy to see this fine volume in print."

-Helen de la Ree

"THE OUTLANDISH ART OF MAHLON BLAINE is an incredible and widely varied collection of a unique artist with a distinctive, gritty style. Many of Blaine's works create a delightfully creepy effect."
-Alan M. Clark

Author and illustrator; Winner of The Deathrealm Award, The International Horror Critic's Guild Award, 4 A.S.F.A. Chesley Awards, World Fantasy for Best Dark Fantasy four time winner, World Fantasy Best Body of Work, and World Fantasy Best Artist (the Howard).

www.ingramcontent.com/pod-product-compliance
Lightning Source LLC
Chambersburg PA
CBHW022126170526
45157CB00004B/1773